ETHIOPIAN
COOKBOOK

PINNACLE OF TRADITIONAL CUISINE

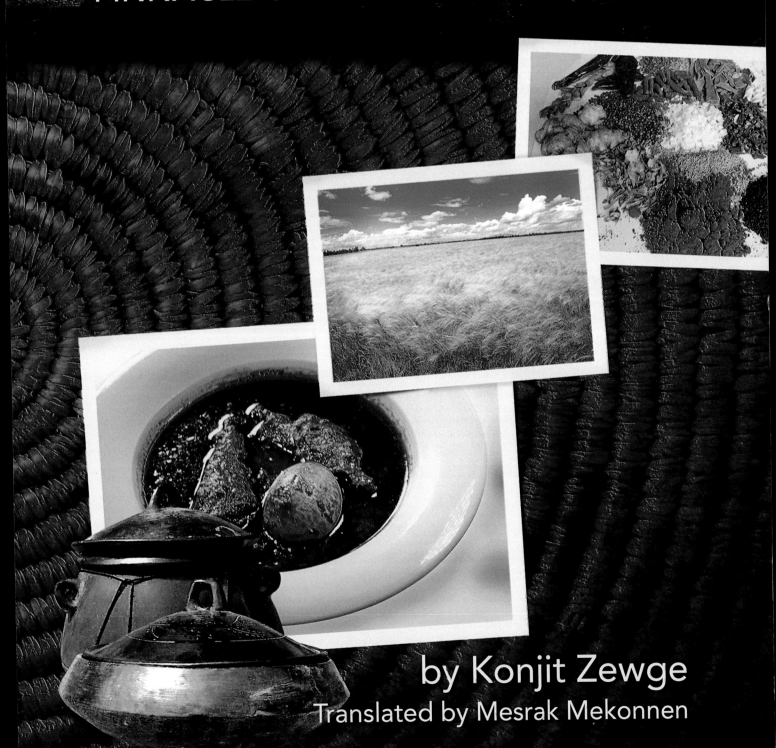

by Konjit Zewge

Translated by Mesrak Mekonnen

ETHIOPIAN COOKBOOK

PINNACLE OF TRADITIONAL CUISINE

by Konjit Zewge

Copyright © 2015 by Konjit Zewge. 717400

ISBN: Softcover   978-1-5035-9042-7
        Hardcover   978-1-5035-9043-4
        EBook   978-1-5035-9041-0

Print information available on the last page

Rev. date: 08/29/2015

To order additional copies of this book, contact:
Xlibris
1-888-795-4274
www.Xlibris.com
Orders@Xlibris.com

ACKNOWLEDGMENT

Mom's Words in Brief

I would like to extend my heartfelt appreciation to my daughter Tiyinte Selassie Mekonnen who encouraged me to write this Ethiopian cook book.

My thanks goes out to my children Mesrak Mekonnen, Nikodimos Mekonnen, Getabecha Mekonnen, Asseged Fisseha and Tosta Selassie Asseged for their various supports.

Thank you Debritu Gebeyehu, Wellansa Shifferaw and Senaite Shifferaw for helping me edit this book and for making my job that much easier and full of fun in Oakland, California.

Ato Melakeselam Yeteshawork and Lulit Melakeselam, thank you for your valuable views and insight generously given while in Denver, Colorado.

DEDICATION

To my beloved, unforgettable sister, Weyzero Kefeye Zwge who has played a crucial role in my formidable years and has always been there for me.

INTRODUCTION

My Mom, at the age of 89, documented her succulent dishes in her book "Yemouya Kouncho". She wrote her book for the sole purpose of passing the art of preparing traditional Ethiopian cuisine to the next generation.

Her parents' home was always filled with extended family, neighbors, and other visitors who delighted in the savoy dishes.

Running the household was traditionally the women's job and learning how to prepare food started at an early age.

As a child, Mom observed her older sisters learn the art of cooking. She could hardly wait until she was old enough to start training. Instructions were done in stages. It started with simple tasks such as washing, dicing, and cutting meat and vegetables. Next, little by little under the watchful eyes of the experts, she was allowed to do more of the cooking. When she was able to prepare meals on her own, it was graduation time.

As an ardent student, Mom made it a point to write down procedures, the various ingredients and amount used in recipes. After she got married, Mom experimented with different amounts of the ingredients and different techniques. She never gave up until she felt the flavors were excellent.

Ethiopian dishes are usually prepared in stew forms and almost always served with "injera". The main ingredients are meat, grains, and legumes. Red meat and chicken are prepared with butter, while fish, legumes, and grain dishes are prepared with oil. The amount of ingredients can be adjusted to ones taste, especially the "berbere" for spicy dishes.

Mom has written the dishes she loved to prepare and serve. As she expressed it in her book, it is her sincere hope that you will enjoy cooking and serving these unique dishes as much as she does.

Mom's cookbook includes more dishes, traditional health drinks, and ingredients preparations. I translated most of the dishes and left the rest for future translation.

Weizero Laketch Tsota

Konjit Zewge

ETHIOPIAN
COOKBOOK
PINNACLE OF TRADITIONAL CUISINE

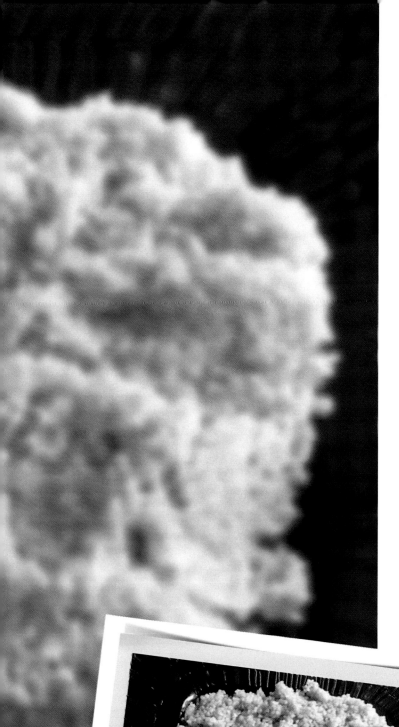

BREAKFAST DISHES

1
ANEBABERO

Note: This recipe calls for mixing a commercially available bread starter with flour and seasonings one day ahead of cooking.

INGREDIENTS

- 2 kg (4 lbs. 6 oz.) teff or whole wheat flour
- 3 tablespoons bread starter (available at a bakery)
- ¼ teaspoon fenugreek
- ¼ teaspoon salt
- Water to mix to pancake batter consistency

PREPARATION

- Mix tef or wheat flour, fenugreek, and salt in a container.
- Add lukewarm water to make a paste.
- Add bread starter.
- Cover and place in a warm area until double in size (depends on warmth of the area – this may take 12 hours or more).
- After 12 hours or so, check to see whether the paste has risen to double its original size. If not, wait until it rises.
- Risen thickness should have a consistency of pancake batter (not very thick).
- If paste is too thick, add lukewarm water and stir.

ABSEET PREPARATION

- Bring 1 ½ cup of cold water to a boil on high heat, then lower the heat to medium high.
- Add 1 ¼ cup of the paste created earlier and stir continuously.
- When it starts to bubble, remove from heat.
- Let it cool.
- Mix with the rest of the paste.
- Keep in a warm place until the dough rises.

BAKING

- Place a frying pan or skillet on medium high heat.
- When the pan is hot, pour the paste like pancake batter.
- Cover with a lid for about one minute.
- Remove the lid. The paste should have holes all over it, like bread.
- Remove from heat and place on a flat surface.
- In the same way, bake a second anebabero.
- Place on a flat surface.
- Take the first anebabero and place it upside down on a flat surface.
- Cover the side that is up now with a thin layer of paste.
- Place the second anebabero with the no-holes side on top of the first anebabero.
- Repeat the same process until paste is used up.
- Cut into smaller sizes to serve.
- If desired, a small amount of Berbere paste can be added to the paste used to stick the two anebaberos together.

Serves 4 to 6 people.

Note: Anebabero can be served any time of the day with coffee or tea.

2

FALSE BANANA ROOTS POWDER DISH
Yeboula Genfo

INGREDIENTS

- 1 cup false banana roots flour (powder)
- 100 grams (3.5 oz.) sweet butter
- 1 cup water
- 1 ¼ cups milk
- Salt (to taste)

FALSE BANANA ROOTS FLOUR PREPARATION

- Mix water and milk in a container.
- Mix the flour with ¼ cup of the water in a container.

COOKING

- Place a heavy pot on medium high heat.
- Add the powder mixture to the pot.
- Add 30 grams (about 2 tablespoons) of butter to the pot.
- Stir continually.
- When the new mixture thickens, fold several times with the spoon.
- When the banana roots powder becomes like dough, make a hole at the center and add ¼ cup of the milk and water mixture.
- Add 33 grams (about 2 tablespoons) butter.

- Cover with a lid and cook on low heat.
- When milk and water mixture is half absorbed, fold the dough several times.
- Make a ball of the yeboula genfo and make a hole at the center.
- Add ¼ cup of milk and water mixture and the remaining butter.
- Cover with lid and bring the milk and water to a low boil (bubbling).
- Remove the lid and fold the yeboula genfo several times.
- Add salt.
- Remove from heat and serve.

Serves 4 to 6 people.

Note: This dish can be served for lunch and dinner.

3

CRACKED WHEAT / BARLEY / CORN DISHES
Yesinde/Yegebse/ Yebekolo kinche

INGREDIENTS

- 1 cup cracked corn
- 100 grams (3.5 oz.) clarified butter
- ½ cup milk
- Salt (to taste)

COOKING

- Place a pot on medium heat.
- Add water, milk, ½ tablespoon clarified butter, and milk to pot and mix together.
- Boil.
- Add wheat, barley, or corn with half of the remaining butter.
- Stir slowly to mix and cover with a lid.
- Lower heat and cook for 10 minutes.
- Reduce heat and cook for another 10 minutes, making sure to stir occasionally.

- Add the remaining butter.
- Check if cracked corn is ready (it will be softened).
- If it is not ready, add more water and cook a while longer, repeating if necessary until done.
- Add salt.
- Remove from heat and serve.

Serves 4 to 5 people.

Note: This dish can be served for lunch and dinner.

4

GARBANZO FLOUR PITA
Yeshimbra Keta

INGREDIENTS

- 125 grams (4.4 oz.) garbanzo flour
- 1 leveled teaspoon Berbere powder
- 2 teaspoons cooking oil
- ¾ cup water
- Salt (to taste)

PREPARATION

- Mix garbanzo flour, Berbere powder, salt, and cooking oil together in a bowl.
- Pour in the water and mix well.

BAKING

- Place a frying pan on medium high heat.
- When the pan is warm, pour in the mixture and spread it to the edge of pan.
- The thickness of the mixture on the pan should be like a crepe.
- Bake on both sides.
- When it becomes crisp, remove from heat and serve

Serves 2 to 3 people.
Note: This dish can be served as snack.

5

GENFO

INGREDIENTS

- 150 grams (5.3 oz.) genfo powder
- 85 grams (3 oz.) clarified butter
- 4 ¼ cups warm water
- 1 tablespoon Berbere paste
- Salt (to taste)

BERBERE PASTE AND BUTTER PREPARATION

- Make Berbere paste (see Glossary).
- In a pan, warm 40 grams (1.4 oz.) clarified butter
- Mix the Berbere paste and warmed butter.

COOKING

- Place a heavy pot on high heat.
- Add 1 ½ cup warm water.
- When water is about to boil, add 5 grams (⅓ tablespoon) clarified butter and salt.
- Sprinkle genfo powder while stirring continuously with a wooden spoon to keep lumps from forming.
- Use the spoon to mix and stir the dough, holding the pot handle with one had while mixing.
- The consistency of genfo will be the same as bread dough.
- With the spoon, make a hole at the center of the genfo and add 15 grams (1 tablespoon) butter.

RECIPE CONTINUED ▶

- Stir or mix well.

- Add ¼ cup warm water and cover with a lid.

- Lower the heat to medium low.

- Let it bubble.

- When water is almost absorbed, stir continuously to keep the genfo from sticking to the bottom of pot.

- If it sticks, add little water and stir it free.

- Add the remaining butter.

- Add ¼ cup warm water and stir to keep lumps from forming.

- If lumps form, remove the pot from heat

- Remove lumps, purée and return the pot to the stove.

- Cover and bring the water to a low boil (bubbling).

- Stir and mix well.

- The genfo should be like bread dough.

- Remove from heat and place on a serving dish.

- Make it look like a round loaf of bread

- Make a hole with a spoon at the center and pour in the Berbere paste with butter.

- Serve.

Serves 2 to 4 people.

Note: This dish is traditionally served when a woman has given birth and people come to visit.

6
TEF CHECHEBSA

INGREDIENTS

- 500 grams (1 lbs. 1 oz.) white or brown tef

- 100 grams (3.5 oz.) clarified butter

- 20 grams (1 ⅓ tablespoon) Berbere paste

- ½ cup cold water

- Salt (to taste)

PREPARATION OF TEFF

- Mix teff and salt in a bowl.

- Add water and mix well with hands to make a thick paste

BERBERE PASTE AND BUTTER PREPARATION

- Place Berbere paste in a small container.

- Add the butter.

- Mix well with the Berbere paste.

COOKING

- Place a frying pan or a skillet on high heat.

- When the pan is heated, add the tef paste.

- Cover the pan by spreading the dough with the bottom of a spoon.

- The thickness of the dough should be similar to a pita.

- Cook on both sides by flipping over for about three minutes on each side on medium heat.

- Remove from heat.

- When it cools, break in small pieces into a bowl.

RECIPE CONTINUED ▶

- Add in the Berebere paste and butter mixture.

- Rub well with hands so that the Berbere mixture is soaked into the pita.

- Set it aside for at least for 10 minutes.

- Warm on a frying pan and serve.

Serves 4 to 6 people.

Note: This dish can be served as snack any time of the day with coffee or tea. Sugar can be also sprinkled on it before eating.

7

WHEAT FLOUR CHECHEBSA

INGREDIENTS

- 300 grams (10.6 oz.) wheat flour

- 50 grams (1.8 oz.) clarified butter

- 20 grams (0.8 oz.) Berbere paste

- Salt (to taste)

- ¼ cup water

FLOUR PREPARATION

- Mix wheat flour and salt in a bowl.

- Add water to the mixture to make a thick paste or dough.

BERBERE PASTE AND BUTTER PREPARATION

- Place Berebere paste (see Glossary) in a bowl.

- Place butter in a pot and melt on low heat.

- Add the melted butter to the bowl and mix well with the Berbere paste.

COOKING

- Place a frying pan or a skillet on high heat.

- When pan is warm, add the paste.

- Spread paste up to the sides of pan to make a thin pita.

- Flip to the other side and cook on each side for about 2 minutes, until done.

- Remove from heat.

- Let it cool.

RECIPE CONTINUED ▶

- Cut into small pieces and place in a bowl.
- Place the Berbere paste and butter mixture in the bowl.
- Rub well into the pita so that the Berbere paste and butter mixture is soaked into the pita pieces.
- Warm on a pan when ready to serve.

Serves 4 to 6 people.

Note: This dish can be served as snack food any time of the day with coffee or tea. Sugar can be sprinkled on it when served.

SPICY SHIRO BREAD DISH

INGREDIENTS

- 55 grams (1.9 oz.) garbanzo flour
- 1 ½ teaspoon awaze
- ½ teaspoon cardamom
- ⅛ teaspoon turmeric
- ¼ cup cooking oil
- ¾ cup water
- salt (to taste)

COOKING

- Mix all ingredients except cardamom.
- Place a pot on medium heat and add the water.
- Add mixture to the pot.
- Stir constantly until the mixture gets thick; its consistency should a bit less thick than bread dough.

BAKING

- Place a heavy frying on medium heat.
- When the pan is warm, add the mixture.
- Stretch the dough to the edge of the pan and bake until the side is done.
- Flip the dough to the second side and bake until it is done.
- Sprinkle cardamom.
- Remove from heat.

Serves 2 people.

ETHIOPIAN BREADS
DABO

17

1

SPICY AND MILD BREAD
Boure Dabo

INGREDIENTS

- 1 kilo (2lbs. 3 oz.) semolina
- 2 kilos (4 lbs. 6 oz.) whole wheat flour
- 2 teaspoons dry yeast
- 2 teaspoons salt
- 1 tablespoon garlic/ginger paste
- 1 tablespoon awaze
- ½ teaspoon cardamom
- 25 grams (about 2 tablespoons) finely minced shallot
- 2 cups seasoned oil (see Glossary, and "Preparation" below)
- 3 cups warm water

SEASONED OIL PREPARATION

- Place pot on medium heat.
- Add shallots and cover with lid.
- Remove lid when steam starts to come out.
- Start stirring and sautéing until good aroma arises.
- Add 1 ½ cup oil and continue sautéing.
- Add garlic/ginger paste and sauté.
- Add awaze and sauté until good aroma arises.
- Add ¼ warm water and sauté until water is absorbed.
- Add another ½ cup of warm water and sauté until water is absorbed.

- Reduce heat to low.
- Keep cooking until the sauce is thickened and oil surfaces.
- Add cardamom and let it settle for a while.
- This oil needs to be strained before use; discard what is on left on the sieve.

BAKING PAN PREPARATION

- Place false banana leaves on all sides and the bottom of several bread baking pans.
- Aluminum (baking) foil can be substituted for the leaves.

DOUGH PREPARATION

- Mix the dry ingredients together.
- Mix 1 cup of warm water with the seasoned oil.
- Divide the mixed flour into two parts.
- Gradually add the seasoned oil to half of the flour and knead.
- Knead and fold several times until dough is smooth and elastic.
- If dough is too dry and thick, add warm water.
- When the dough becomes smooth and elastic, stop adding the seasoned oil (you may discard the unused amount).
- Make a ball with the dough and place in a container in a warm area. Cover it.
- When dough rises, knead again for a few minutes and cover.
- Let it rise another time.
- Place half of the flour mixture in another container.
- Prepare the dough in the same manner.
- The only difference for this part of dough is that seasoned oil is not added.

RECIPE CONTINUED ▶

BAKING

- Preheat oven to 400 degrees Fahrenheit.

- Divide the white dough into two parts.

- Place one part on the pan.

- Divide the dough with seasoned oil into three parts.

- Take a third of the dough and divide it into equal parts, making two balls.

- Flatten the balls of dough to be between one-half inch and one inch thick.

- Place the white dough that is in the pan into two different spots.

- Layer with the white dough, extending to the edges of the pan, to create a red-white pattern.

- Place the dough with seasoned oil on top of the white dough, extending to the edges of the pan.

- Cover with false banana leaves and let the dough rise.

- Bake in oven for one hour, then CHECK to see if it is ready by pricking it with a toothpick. If the toothpick pulls out dry, the bread is done.

- If dough is not ready, the pick will have dough on it. If so, bake a while longer and test again. Different ovens may vary the baking time.

- When bread is ready, remove it from the oven and let it stand until cooled.

- Place cooled bread upside down (to keep it from crumbling) on a cutting board and cut with a knife or break with your hands.

This recipe typically serves 15 to 20 people.

2

SPICY BREAD
Key Dabo

INGREDIENTS

- 1 kilo (2.2 lbs.) semolina or wheat flour
- 2 ½ cups cooking oil (for making seasoned oil. See Glossary and "Preparation" below)
- 1 teaspoon garlic/ginger paste
- ½ teaspoon cardamom
- 1 ¾ cup warm water
- 2 kilos (4.4 lbs.) wheat flour
- 2 teaspoons salt
- 2 teaspoons dry yeast
- 1 cup awaze
- 25 grams (about 2 tablespoons) finely minced shallot
- 2 ½ cups seasoned oil
- 1 teaspoon cardamom
- 1 ¾ cups warm water

AWAZE SAUCE PREPARATION

- Place pot on medium heat.
- Add shallots and cover with lid.
- Remove lid when steam starts to come out.
- Start stirring and sautéing until good aroma rises.
- Add oil and continue to sauté for a little while
- Add garlic/ginger paste and sauté.
- Add awaze and sauté until good aroma arises.
- Add ¼ cup warm water and sauté until water is absorbed.

- Add another ½ cup of warm water and sauté until water is absorbed.
- Reduce heat to low.
- Keep cooking until the sauce is thickened and oil surfaces.
- Add cardamom and let it settle for a while.
- Strain to use the seasoned oil, discarding what is on left on the sieve.

BAKING PAN PREPARATION

- Place false banana leaves on the sides and at the bottom of several bread baking pans.
- Aluminum (baking) foil can be substituted for the leaves.

DOUGH PREPARATION

- Mix semolina, flour, salt and dry yeast together.
- Mix 1 cup warm water with the seasoned oil.
- Mix the dough, gradually adding the mixed water and seasoned oil.
- Knead and fold until dough is smooth and elastic.
- When dough is smooth and elastic, stop kneading.
- If dough is too thick or dry, add some more warm water.
- When the dough becomes smooth and elastic, stop adding the seasoned oil (you may discard the unused amount).
- Make a ball with the dough and place it in a container.
- Cover container and place it in a warm area to let it rise until double.
- When dough rises, knead again for a few minutes and cover.
- Cover the container and keep it in the same place for the dough to rise again.

RECIPE CONTINUED ▶

TRADITIONAL ETHIOPIAN COOKBOOK

BAKING

- Preheat oven to 400 degrees Fahrenheit.

- Cover the pan with false banana leaves or foil and place the dough into the pan.

- Place in the oven for one hour, then test to see if it is ready by pricking it with a toothpick. If the toothpick pulls out dry, the bread is done.

- If dough is not ready, the pick will have dough on it. If so, bake a while longer and test again. Different ovens may vary the baking time.

- When bread is ready, remove it from the oven and let it stand until cooled.

- Place cooled bread upside down (to keep it from crumbling) on a cutting board and cut with a knife or break with your hands.

Serves 6 to 8 people.

TRADITIONAL ETHIOPIAN COOKBOOK

3

WHITE BREAD
Nech Dabo

INGREDIENTS

- 2 kilos (4 lbs. 6 oz.) semolina
- 3 kilos (6 lbs. 10 oz.) whole wheat flour
- 4 level teaspoons salt
- 5 teaspoons dry yeast
- 3 cups cooking oil
- 3 cups warm water

DOUGH PREPARATION

- Mix all dry ingredients.
- Mix warm water with oil.
- Gradually add water and oil into flour mixture while kneading.
- Knead and fold dough several times until mixture is finished.
- Stop kneading when dough is smooth and elastic.
- If dough is too thick and dry when the water and oil mixture is finished, add some warm water.
- If dough is smooth and elastic without using all of the water and oil mixture, discard the remainder of the liquid.

BAKING

- Roll dough into a ball and place into a large container.
- Cover container and place in warm area to let the dough rise.

- When the dough rises, knead it.
- Let it rise again.
- Preheat the oven to 400 degrees Fahrenheit.
- Place the dough in a bread baking pans that hold 2 pounds or smaller.
- Cover with false banana leaves, or use aluminum (baking) foil as a substitute for the leaves.
- Place in oven for one hour, then test to see if it is ready by pricking it with a toothpick. If the toothpick pulls out dry, the bread is done.
- If dough is not ready, the pick will have dough on it. If so, bake a while longer and test again. Different ovens may vary the baking time.
- When bread is ready, remove it from the oven and let it stand until cooled.
- Place cooled bread upside down (to keep it from crumbling) on a cutting board and cut with a knife or break with your hands.

Serves 6 to 8 people.

YETENSIS BREAD
Yetensis Dabo

Note: This recipe requires soaking wheat kernels in water for 12 hours, then sprouting them for a day, and drying them in a sunny spot. After this is ground and mixed with other ingredients, it needs to sit in a warm spot for 3 days.

INGREDIENTS

- 4 kilograms and 200 grams (9 lbs. 4 oz.) whole wheat flour
- 2 ½ teaspoons salt
- 1 handful lemon grass
- 3 cups cooking oil
- 3 garlic cloves
- 1 cup wheat kernels for tensis (see preparation below)
- 8 cups cold water
- 3 cups *tej* (Ethiopian honey wine)

TENSIS PREPARATION

- Rinse the wheat kernels with cold water.
- Place the wheat in a container and cover with cold water in a cold place for 12 hours.
- Drain water.
- Pack the wheat kernels tightly back in the container and stand for a day.
- Once the kernels have sprouted, spread them out in a sunny place to dry.
- Grind the dry kernels to the size of cracked wheat.

- Separate the cracked wheat from the flour that is formed when grinding; discard the flour.
- Wash the cracked wheat with cold water.
- To the rinsed cracked wheat, add 2 cups of tej, 6 cups of water, and the lemon grass.
- Keep in a warm place for three days.
- Strain and save the water mixture in a different container.
- Rub the cracked wheat between both hands.
- Add the strained water mixture back into the cracked wheat.
- Separate the liquid back into the different container again.
- Repeat the process one more time, until the coating or skin is separated from the wheat
- Strain the wheat skin off through a sieve and discard.

BREAD PREPARATION

- Place 200 grams (7 oz.) whole wheat flour in a bowl.
- Add water to make thin dough.
- Place a frying pan on high heat.
- Pour dough onto the heated pan.
- Fry on both sides until it is golden brown; the thickness of dough should be similar to pita bread.
- When the bread is ready, cut into small pieces.
- Place the cut pieces into the tensis and rub.
- Strain and keep the liquid part in a container and leave cut bread pieces, on sieve.
- Place sieve over another container.
- Add some of the liquid back on the sieve and rub cut bread pieces (kita).
- Mix both liquid parts.
- Add 2 cups of water to the tensis.
- Discard what is left on sieve.

RECIPE CONTINUED ▶

DOUGH PREPARATION

- Place 2 kilos (4 lbs. 6.4 oz.) whole wheat flour in a large container.

- Mix with the tensis and rub and fold several times.

- If dough is too thick, add needed amount of lukewarm water and mix well.

- Add 1 cup tej and mix.

- When dough is smooth and elastic, add the 3 whole cloves of garlic after placing them on toothpicks for easy removal later.

- Cover the container and place in a warm location.

- Dough should rise in 2 hours.

- If dough does not rise, add dry yeast into the remaining bread flour

- Add oil and salt to the flour and mix.

- Combine dough in both containers

- If dough has risen in 2 hours do not add yeast, but add the flour, oil, and salt.

- If dough becomes dry, add needed amount of lukewarm water.

- Keep in warm place to rise.

BAKING PAN PREPARATION

- Cover bottom and sides of a baking pan with false banana leaves, or use aluminum (baking) foil as a substitute for the leaves.

BAKING

- Place the dough in the lined baking pan and cover with false banana leaves or foil.

- Let the dough rise on the baking pan.

- Place in an oven that has been preheated to 400 degrees Fahrenheit.

- Place in oven for one hour, then test to see if it is ready by pricking it with a toothpick. If the toothpick pulls out dry, the bread is done.

- If bread is not ready, there will be dough on the toothpick. If so, bake a while longer and test again.

- When bread is ready, remove it from the oven and let it stand until cooled.

- Place cooled bread upside down (to keep it from crumbling) on a cutting board and cut with a knife or break with your hands.

Serves 6 to 8 people.

5

INJERA

Note: This recipe calls for making ersho three days ahead of mixing the other ingredients. Once mixed, the bread dough must sit for four days.

INGREDIENTS

- 1 kilogram (2 lbs. 3 oz.) white or brown injera flour
- 2 tablespoons ersho (see below)
- 3 cups water

ERSHO PREPARATION

- Three days before baking injera, mix 3 tablespoons of tej (Ethiopian honey wine) with 1 cup of water.
- Cover and keep for later use.

INJERA DOUGH PREPARATION

- Place injera flour in a large container.
- Add a little amount of water and rub the flour with both hands.
- Repeat the same process until all the water is completely used.
- If the paste is not thin, add more water (beyond the 3 cups listed).
- Add the prepared ersho and mix well.
- Keep in a warm place for four days.

DOUGH PREPARATION

- Pour out water surfacing from the dough that has sat for four days.
- Add 1 cup water to thin the injera mix.
- Remove 2 tablespoons of the mix into a small bowl to use later.

ABSEET PREPARATION

- Place a pot on medium heat.
- Add ¼ cup water.
- When water gets warm, add the 2 tablespoons saved injera mixture.
- Stir quickly while over the heat to keep the mixture from forming lumps.
- When it starts to bubble, remove from heat and cool.
- Mix the ingredients from the pan into the main portion of the injera dough or paste.
- Cover and keep in a warm place for the dough to rise.

RECIPE CONTINUED ▶

TRADITIONAL ETHIOPIAN COOKBOOK

BAKING

- Place a coated pan or pancake baking pan on medium heat.

- Pour about ½ cup of dough into the pan.

- Move the pan in a circular motion to spread the dough to the edges of the pan.

- Cover for about one minute.

- Injera is ready when small holes appear all over the surface and along the injera's edge.

- The injera will start to curl up or rise from the pan.

- Remove from pan and place on a flat surface.

- Repeat the same process until dough is used up.

- Do not place one injera on top of the other until it cools down.

Each pan of cooked injera serves 1 person.

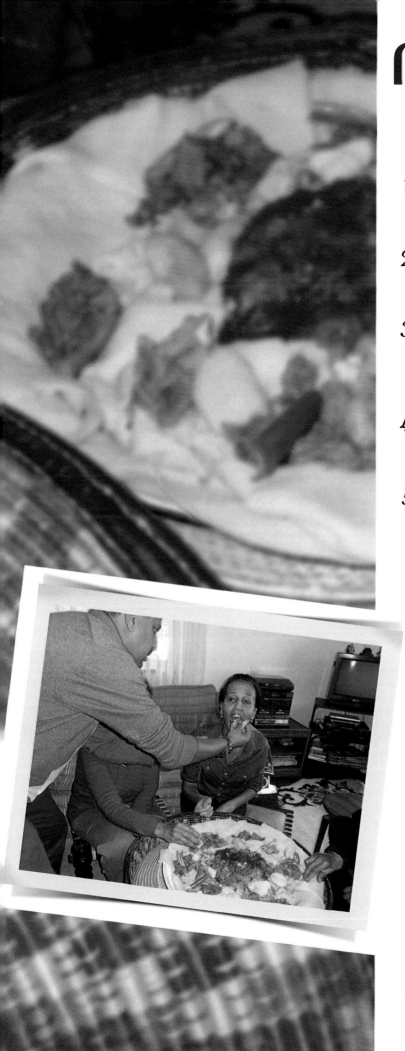

MILD MEAT DISHES

1

BEEF OR
LAMB DISH
Yebere or Beg Alicha

INGREDIENTS

- 300 grams (10.6 oz.) beef or lamb meat (some with bones)
- 300 grams (10.6 oz.) finely minced shallots
- 270 grams (9.5 oz.) clarified butter
- 3 cups water
- 1 tablespoon garlic/ginger paste
- 4 jalapeños or Serrano peppers
- ⅛ teaspoon turmeric (optional)
- salt (to taste)

PREPARATION

- Wash meat with cold water and strain.

COOKING

- Place a heavy pot on medium heat.
- Add shallots and cover with lid.
- Remove lid when steam starts to rise and begin to stir.
- Sauté for 10 minutes until a good aroma arises.
- Add butter and sauté for 10 minutes.
- Add ½ tablespoon garlic/ginger paste and cook for five minutes.
- Add meat and sauté for 15 minutes and when a good aroma rises, add 1 cup water.

- Increase heat to medium high.
- Let the sauce bubble for 10 minutes.
- Repeat the same process two times.
- Add the remaining garlic/ginger paste.
- Add turmeric.
- Lower heat to medium and stir occasionally for five minutes.
- Check if meat is tender. If it is not tender, add ¼ cup water and cook until it is tender.
- When meat is done and sauce has thickened, add salt.
- Lower heat to simmer.
- When butter surfaces, remove from heat.

Serves 4 to 6 people.

2

BEEF OR LAMB TRIPE DISH

Eskenfour Alecha

INGREDIENTS

- 400 grams (14.1 oz.) beef or lamb tripe
- 200 grams (7 oz.) lean minced meat
- 250 grams (8.8 oz.) finely minced shallots
- 220 grams (7.7 oz.) clarified butter
- 1 tablespoon garlic/ginger paste
- 2 tablespoon afrenge (jalapeño seed and seasoning mixture – see Glossary)
- 30 grams (1 oz.) shinkourt kimem (spice mixture)
- 20 grams (0.8 oz.) ginger paste
- 1 teaspoon white pepper
- salt (to taste)
- ¼ teaspoon cumin
- ½ teaspoon cardamom
- 3 garlic cloves, puréed
- 3 jalapeños or Serrano peppers
- ¼ cup tej (Ethiopian honey wine)
- 2 cups water
- Cheesecloth for straining broth

GARLIC/GINGER PASTE PREPARATION

- Mix the garlic/ginger paste with ¼ cup tej

STUFFING PREPARATION

- Mix 200 grams (7 oz.) minced lean beef meat with the following ingredients:
- 1 teaspoon white pepper
- 30 grams (1 oz.) shenkourt kimem
- 3 puréed garlic cloves
- 20 grams (1 ⅓ tablespoon) ginger paste
- ½ leveled teaspoon cardamom
- 3 jalapeños or Serrano peppers, finely minced
- salt (to taste)

AFRENGE BROTH PREPARITION

- Mix afrenge with ¼ cup water.
- Add ¾ cup of water and mix well, then let it stand for three minutes.
- Strain the afrenge into a container.
- Place what is left on the sieve into another container, then add ¼ cup of water and mix well.
- Add another ½ cup of water and mix well, let stand for three minutes and strain.
- Mix the broth in the two containers.
- Place what is on the sieve into a separate container.
- Add ¾ cup of water and mix well, then let it stand for 10 minutes and strain with cloth.
- Mix the two broths together, and discard what remains on the cloth.

TRIPE PREPARATION

- If tripe was already cleaned when purchased, rinse several times with cold water.
- For tripe that needs to be cleaned, wash the tripe with cold water several times until the pungent smell is gone.

RECIPE CONTINUED ▶

- Cut into rectangular pieces 5 cm by 12 cm (about 2 inches by 5 inches), then keep in cold water.

- Boil water in a pan, using enough to cover the pieces of tripe.

- Dip each cut piece of tripe into the boiling water, honeycomb side down, for 30 seconds.

- Place the piece honeycomb side up on a cutting board.

- Scrape with a knife to remove the dark layer, then flip the piece over and scrape the thin filament.

- Rinse the pieces twice with cold water and strain.

TRIPE POCKET

- Place a piece of tripe on a cutting board with the honeycomb side down.

- Fold the piece over once into equal sides, then sew together on two sides with thread and needle to make the pocket.

STUFFING THE POCKETS

- Place the prepared stuffing mixture in each pocket; avoid over-filling to keep the pockets from bursting.

- Close the opening by sewing the third side with a needle and thread.

COOKING

- Place a heavy pot on medium heat.

- Add shallots and cover with lid.

- When steam starts to escape, remove lid and start to sauté.

- When shallots seem to wilt and become glossy, add butter.

- Add garlic/ginger paste and tej mixture.

- Sauté for 15 minutes, and when a good aroma arises, add the tripe pockets.

- Continue to sauté for 15 minutes.

- Add 1 cup of afrenge broth, cover and let it boil until the liquid is reduced.

- Repeat the same procedure until afrenge broth is used.

- Check the tripe to determine if it has become tender.

- If the tripe is ready before all the broth is used, discard the extra broth.

- Add the remaining garlic/ginger paste and tej mixture.

- Add cumin.

- Cook on low heat until the sauce becomes medium thick.

- Lower heat to simmer and add salt to taste.

- Remove from heat when the butter starts to surface.

Serves 4 to 6 people.

3

BEEF OR LAMB DISH WITH OR WITHOUT TOMATOS
Yebere or Beg Tematimalicha

INGREDIENTS

- 300 grams (10.6 oz.) beef or lamb meat (some with bones)
- 1 tablespoon garlic/ginger paste
- ⅛ teaspoon turmeric (optional)
- 4 jalapeño or Serrano peppers
- 200 grams (7 oz.) finely minced shallots
- 200 grams (7 oz.) clarified butter
- 4 ripe Roma tomatoes
- 1 tablespoon tomato paste
- 3 cups water
- salt (to taste)

PREPARATION

- Wash meat with cold water and strain.
- Wash tomatoes, and chop if desired.

COOKING

- Place a heavy pot on medium heat.
- Add shallots and cover with lid.
- Remove lid when steam starts to rise and stir.
- Sauté for 10 minutes until a good aroma arises.

- Add butter and sauté for 10 minutes.
- Add ½ tablespoon garlic/ginger paste and cook for five minutes.
- Add tomatoes and sauté until is liquid is almost absorbed.
- Add tomato paste and sauté for about 10 minutes.
- Add meat and sauté for 15 minutes and when a good aroma rises, add 1 cup water.
- Increase heat to medium high and let the sauce bubble for 10 minutes.
- Repeat the same process two times, adding 1 cup of water each time.
- Add the remaining garlic/ginger paste.
- Lower heat to medium and stir occasionally for five minutes.
- Check if meat is tender. If it is not tender, add ¼ cup water and cook a while longer.
- When meat is done and sauce has thickened, add salt.
- Lower heat to simmer.
- When butter surfaces, remove from heat.

Serves 4 to 6 people.

4

CHICKEN DISH
Yedoro Alicha

INGREDIENTS

- 1 whole chicken
- 1 whole lime
- 12 hard boiled eggs, shells removed
- 350 grams (12.3 oz.) finely minced shallots
- 300 grams (10.6 oz.) clarified butter
- 1 tablespoon garlic/ginger paste
- Salt (to taste)
- 1 teaspoon mastekakeya kimem (spice)
- ½ teaspoon yetom alicha derek kimem (spice)
- 100 grams (3.5 oz.) Berbere paste
- 2 ½ cups warm water
- 1 teaspoon cardamom
- 2 peppers, jalapeños or Serrano

CHICKEN PREPARATION

- Skin chicken and cut it into pieces.
- Scrape off yellow fatty substance with knife and dispose.
- Cut lime and place in cold water for rinsing the chicken.
- Wash several times in the water until chicken is odorless.

COOKING

- Place pot on medium heat.
- Add shallots to pot and cover with lid.

- When steam starts to come out, remove lid and stir shallots for about five minutes.
- Add ¼ cup of water and put on lid.
- When water bubbles, remove lid and sauté until water is almost absorbed.
- Add butter and sauté for 15 minutes.
- Add ½ tablespoon garlic/ginger paste and cook while stirring for five minutes.
- Add chicken pieces.
- Add ½ cup of warm water and have the sauce bubble for five minutes.
- Repeat the same process one more time.
- Add the remaining garlic/ginger paste and cook for two minutes.
- Add yetom alicha derek kimem and jalapeño or Serrano peppers.
- Cook on low heat until sauce thickens for about 15 minutes.
- Check if meat is done. If chicken is not done, add ¼ cup of water and cook until done.
- When meat is done, add whole eggs and cook for two minutes to heat all ingredients.
- Lower heat to simmer.
- When butter surfaces, remove from heat.

Serves 4 to 6 people

5

TRIPE DISH
Cheguara Kikle

INGREDIENTS

- 600 grams (1lbs. 5 oz.) tripe
- 200 grams (7 oz.) finely minced shallots
- 100 grams (3.5 oz.) clarified butter
- 2 teaspoons garlic/ginger paste
- 5 jalapeño or Serrano peppers
- Water
- pinch of turmeric
- salt (to taste)

TRIPE PREPARATION

- If tripe has been already cleaned when purchased, wash with cold water several times.
- For tripe that needs to be cleaned, wash the tripe with cold water several times until the pungent smell is gone.
- Cut into rectangular pieces or cubes and keep in cold water.
- Boil water in a pan.
- Dip each cut piece of tripe into the boiling water, honeycomb side down, for 30 seconds.
- Place the piece honeycomb side up on a cutting board.
- Scrape with a knife to remove the dark layer, then flip the piece over and scrape the thin filament.
- Rinse the pieces twice with cold water and strain.

COOKING

- Place a frying pan on high heat.
- Add shallots and butter, and then sauté.
- When a good aroma arises, add garlic/ginger paste.
- Place tripe pieces and sauté.
- Add ½ cup of water several times until tripe pieces are tender.
- Add jalapeño or Serrano peppers when tripe is half done.
- Cook in medium heat until sauce is medium thick.
- Add turmeric.
- Remove from heat when tripe is done.

Serves 4 to 6 people

ETHIOPIAN COOKBOOK

PINNACLE OF TRADITIONAL CUISINE

MILD VEGETABLE DISHES

1

GARBANZO DISH
Wetecha

INGREDIENTS

- 160 grams (5.6 oz.) garbanzo flour
- 2 tablespoon minced shallots
- 1 tablespoon white pepper
- 1 cup plus 6 tablespoons seasoned oil (see Glossary)
- 2 ¾ cups cold water
- 2 green jalapeños
- 1 red jalapeño
- salt (to taste)

PREPARATION

- Mix garbanzo flour with ¾ cup of the cold water in a bowl.

COOKING

- Place a pot on medium heat.
- Add 2 cups of water.
- Add 2 tablespoons seasoned oil.
- When water starts to bubble, add the garbanzo flour that was mixed with ¾ cup of cold water while stirring constantly.
- Continue to stir on low heat for about five minutes to be sure the garbanzo flour does not stick to the bottom of the pot.
- Add salt.
- Add 4 tablespoons of seasoned oil.
- Cook for 30 minutes on low heat, stirring occasionally.

- Remove from heat.
- Cover and keep in a cool place or refrigerator for 24 hours.
- Remove the top hardened layer and mix the rest with a spoon.
- Slowly add the remaining oil while stirring slowly.
- Chop the jalapeños after removing the seeds.
- Sprinkle the chopped jalapeños on top.
- Sprinkle shallots and white pepper, mix.
- Note: This can be eaten with injera or as a spread on bread.

Serves 4 to 6 people

2

SAFFLOWER DISH
Yesouf Fitfit

Note: This dish is served with injera.

INGREDIENTS

- 180 grams (6.3 oz.) safflower seeds
- 6 garlic cloves
- 6 fresh rue seeds
- 1 little branch of rue
- 7 cups cold water
- salt (to taste)

SAFFLOWER PREPARATION

- Place a pot on high heat and add 3 cups of water.
- Bring the water to a boil.
- Add the safflower seeds and boil until seeds look black in color.
- Remove from heat.
- Sieve the seeds.
- Grind the seeds.
- Place ground safflower in a container.

SAFFLOWER SAUCE PREPARATION

- Add ½ cup of the cold water to the container with the safflower seeds and rub with hands.
- Add another ½ cup of the cold water to the safflower seed sauce and rub with hands again.
- Let it stand for five minutes.
- Sieve the sauce by pouring slowly.

- Place the safflower seeds from the sieve into another container.
- Add the remaining cold water and repeat the same process.
- Discard the safflower seeds from the sieve.
- Mix the two sauces together.
- Add rue seeds, rue branch, and garlic cloves to sauce.
- Add salt.
- When ready to serve, remove the rue seeds, branches, and garlic cloves.
- Cut injera into small pieces and place in a serving dish.
- Pour the safflower sauce over the injera pieces.
- Make sure injera in well soaked with sauce and serve.

Serves 4 to 6 people

3

SAFFLOWER WITH POTATO DISH
Yesouf Alicha

INGREDIENTS

- 120 grams (4.2 oz.) safflower seeds
- 140 grams (5 oz.) finely minced shallots
- 40 grams (1.4 oz.) chopped jalapeños with seeds removed
- 30 grams (1 oz.) alicha shero
- 5 large Idaho potatoes, chopped
- ½ cup plus 5 tablespoons cooking oil
- 7 cups water

SAFFLOWER SEED PREPARATION

- Place a pot on high heat with 3 cups of water.
- Bring the water to a boil.
- Add safflower seeds to the boiling water and cook until the seeds get black in color.
- Remove from heat and strain.
- Grind the seeds and place in a container.
- Add ½ cup water and rub with hands.
- Add another ½ cup of water and rub with hands.
- Let it stand for five minutes.
- Sieve the mixture by pouring slowly.
- Place the seeds from the strainer into another container.
- Repeat the same process once more.
- Discard the seeds on the strainer.
- Mix the sauces together.

ALICHA SHIRO PREPARATION

- Place alicha shiro in a container. Add a little amount of water to make a thin paste. This is done so that alicha shero does not form lumps when added to the cooking pot.

POTATOES

- Peel potatoes and cut them into desired size. Cover with cold water until ready to use.

COOKING

- Place a heavy pot on medium high heat.
- Add the sauce to the pot.
- When it starts to bubble, slowly pour in the alicha shiro paste and stir.
- Wait until it bubbles well and add oil, shallots, and jalapeños.
- Simmer for 15 minutes until the sauce reaches a medium thickness.
- Keep stirring and when oil starts to appear, add the potatoes.
- Lower heat and cook until potatoes are softened.
- Add salt.
- Remove from heat.
- Keep in a cool place or refrigerator.
- Serve cold.

Serves 4 to 6 people

4

SESAME SEED DISH
Yeselit Fetfet

Note: This recipe is served with pieces of injera.

INGREDIENTS

- 170 grams (6 oz.) white or brown sesame seeds
- 2 ¼ cups water

BROWN SESAME SEED PREPARATION

- Place a skillet or frying pan on high heat.
- When warm, add the sesame seeds.
- Sauté until the color becomes darker brown.
- Remove from heat and allow to cool.
- Grind the seeds and place in a container.
- Grind until they become oily.

WHITE SESAME SEEDS PREPARATION

- Place a skillet or frying pan on high heat.
- When warm, add the sesame seeds.
- Sauté until the seeds are hot (be careful the seeds do not get dark).
- Remove from heat and allow to cool.
- Grind the seeds and place in a container.
- Grind until they become oily.

BROWN AND WHITE SESAME SEED PREPARATION

- Add 1¼ cup of water to the sesame seeds and rub with hands.
- Sieve the mixture.
- Place the sesame seeds from the strainer into another bowl.
- Add 1 cup and repeat the process.
- Strain the mixture with a straining cloth (such as a cheese cloth).
- Discard the sieved sesame seeds.
- Mix the two sauces.
- Add salt.
- Let it stand for 10 minutes.
- Sieve again with strainer.
- Prepare a serving dish with small pieces of injera.
- Pour sauce on the injera pieces until all pieces are well soaked.

Serves 4 to 6 people

5

SPLIT CHICK PEA DISH

Yeater Kike Alicha

INGREDIENTS

- 200 grams (7 oz.) dry, split chick peas
- 200 grams (7 oz.) minced shallots
- 1 tablespoon ginger/garlic paste
- 1 tablespoon finely minced garlic
- 1 tablespoon finely minced ginger
- 1 teaspoon yetom alicha derek kimem
- 4 jalapeños or Serrano peppers
- ¾ cup cooking oil
- 4 cups water

SPLIT CHICK PEA PREPARATION

- Wash peas thoroughly with cold water.
- Boil 4 cups of water.
- Add the peas to the boiling water.
- Remove from heat when halfway cooked.
- Drain into a sieve and place into a container, saving the cooking water in a separate bowl for later use.

COOKING

- Mix shallots, minced garlic, and minced ginger in a bowl.
- Place a pot on medium heat.
- Place the mixture in the pot and cover with lid.
- When steam starts to rise, remove the lid.
- Sauté until shallots wilt (do not let shallots get dark in color).
- Add ½ tablespoon of the ginger/garlic paste.
- Cook until a good aroma rises.
- Add chick peas and cook until the peas start to get a little softer.
- Add 1 cup of the saved cooking water.
- Lower heat and sauté.
- Add yetom alicha derek kimem and stir.
- Add 1 cup of the saved water and cook for 10 minutes.
- Add the remaining ginger/garlic paste.
- Add the jalapeños.
- Keep cooking by gradually adding the remaining water until the peas are thoroughly cooked.
- Add salt.
- Lower heat to simmer and cook until the oil surfaces.
- Remove from heat.

Serves 4 to 6 people

6

YESHERO ALICHA

INGREDIENTS

- 60 grams (2.1 oz.) alicha shiro
- 75 grams (2.6 oz.) minced shallots
- 3 chopped jalapeños or Serrano peppers
- ½ tablespoon ginger/garlic paste
- 3 branches of holy basil
- ½ cup cooking oil
- 2 cups warm water
- 2 cups cold water
- salt (to taste)

ALICHA SHIRO PREPARATION

- Place the alicha shiro in a bowl.
- Add a little amount of cold water and stir to make a thin paste (to prevent the alicha shiro from forming lumps when added to the pot later).

COOKING

- Place a pot on medium heat.
- Add shallots and cover with lid.
- When steam starts to rise, remove lid, stir and add oil.
- Sauté until a good aroma rises.
- Add ¼ tablespoon ginger/garlic paste.
- Stir continuously for five minutes.
- Add the cold water and stir.
- When it bubbles, sprinkle the alicha shiro and stir constantly.
- Lower heat and continue to stir until a good aroma rises.
- Add warm water and cook.
- Add basil.
- Lower heat and cover with a lid.
- When shiro foam begins to surface, remove the lid and keep stirring.
- Cook until the flavor of the shiro flour becomes unnoticeable and the flavors are well blended through cooking.
- Lower heat to a simmer.
- When oil starts to surface, sprinkle jalapeños.
- Add salt.
- Remove the basil.
- Remove from heat.

Serves 4 to 6 people

ETHIOPIAN
COOKBOOK
PINNACLE OF TRADITIONAL CUISINE

SPICY MEAT DISHES

1

SPICY ETHIOPIAN BEEF JERKY DISH, TYPE I

Menchetabish Wot

INGREDIENTS

- 120 grams (4.2 oz.) quanta (Ethiopian beef jerky)
- 250 grams (8.8 oz.) finely minced shallots
- 320 grams (11.2 oz.) clarified butter
- 105 grams (3.7 oz.) Berbere paste
- 45 grams (1.6 oz.) nech shero
- 1 ½ tablespoon garlic/ginger paste
- 1 teaspoon cardamom
- 1 teaspoon mastekakeya kimem (spice)
- 1 teaspoon koulet kimem (spice)
- 1 teaspoon fenugreek
- 1 teaspoon cinnamon
- 1 ½ cups dry tej (Ethiopian honey wine)
- 2 ¼ cups water
- salt (to taste)

BEEF JERKY PREPARATION

- Grind the beef jerky into powder by first crushing it in a mortar, then grinding it to powder in a coffee grinder.

PREPARATION

- Mix ¼ cup of dry tej with garlic/ginger paste.
- Mix 1 ½ cup of dry tej with 1 ¼ cups of water.
- Mix nech shiro with additional water to make a thin paste.
- Mix Berbere paste with 1 tablespoon butter.

COOKING

- Place a heavy pot on medium heat.
- Add fenugreek to the center of the pot and sauté until it gets brown.
- Add the minced shallots and sauté for 20 minutes until they wilt and get brownish.
- Add butter, saving 25 grams (just over 1 ½ tablespoon) of butter for later use.
- Stir for about 10 minutes until a good aroma rises.
- Add tej and garlic/ginger mixture and stir for a few minutes.
- Add quanta powder and sauté until good aroma rises.
- Add 1 ¼ cups of tej and water mixture, stirring occasionally and cooking for 10 minutes.
- Add the shiro paste and stir constantly to keep lumps from forming.
- Cook about 15 minutes, until shiro is ready.
- Add Berbere paste and butter and stir.
- Add koulet kimem and stir.
- Keep stirring and cooking for 15 minutes until Berbere paste gets darker in color.
- Taste to determine if Berbere is too hot or has become milder; if Berbere is too hot, pour in an additional ¼ cup of water and cook.
- When Berebere paste is milder, add mastekakeya kimem.
- Add cinnamon.

RECIPE CONTINUED ▶

- Add ½ tablespoon of the remaining garlic/ginger paste and stir constantly.

- Add 1 ¼ cups of tej and water mixture.

- Add 25 grams (just over 1 ½ tablespoon) butter and continue to stir until the sauce thickens.

- Add 1 cup warm water and cook until added water is well mixed with the sauce.

- Add salt.

- Reduce heat to simmer and cook until butter surfaces.

- Sprinkle cardamom and remove from heat.

- Sauce should not be very thick.

Serves 4 to 6 people

2

SPICY ETHIOPIAN BEEF JERKY DISH, TYPE II
Menchetabish Wot

INGREDIENTS

- 120 grams (4.2 oz.) quanta (Ethiopian Beef Jerky)

- 1 teaspoon makoulaya kimem (spice)

- 250 grams (8.8 oz.) finely minced shallots

- 1 teaspoon mastekakeya kimem (spice)

- 290 grams (10.2 oz.) clarified butter

- 1 pinch fenugreek stirred into 1 tablespoon water

- 120 grams (4.2 oz.) Berbere paste

- 1 tablespoon finely minced garlic

- 1 tablespoon finely minced ginger

- 45 grams (1.6 oz.) nech shiro

- 1 ½ tablespoon garlic/ginger paste

- 1 tablespoon shenkourt makulaya (spice)

- 1 teaspoon cardamom

- salt (to taste)

- 1 ½ cups warm water

RECIPE CONTINUED ▶

BEEF JERKY PREPARATION

- Grind the beef jerky into powder by first crushing it in a mortar, then grinding it to powder in a coffee grinder.

COOKING

- Place a heavy pot on medium heat.

- Add shallots, minced garlic, and minced ginger to the pot.

- Cover with lid until steam comes out.

- Remove lid and stir shallots for 20 minutes until they are wilted and they become brown in color.

- If shallots stick to pot while sautéing, push the free shallots away from the sticking area and splash water where the shallots are sticking, then scrape and mix with the other shallots.

- When shallots have completely browned, push them toward the edge to free the center of the pot.

- Add the pinch of fenugreek and sauté until it gets dark in color.

- When fenugreek and water mixture bubbles, add Berbere paste and sauté.

- Repeat this process until the spiciness of the Berbere paste is reduced to mildness.

- Save 25 grams (just over 1 ½ tablespoon) butter and put the rest of the butter in the pot.

- Sauté for 20 minutes until Berbere paste becomes dark in color.

- Add half of the garlic/ginger paste and continue to stir.

- When a good aroma arises, add the quanta powder.

- Add ½ cup warm water.

- Add shiro and stir fast to keep lumps from forming. (To avoid the formation of lumps, mix shiro with cold water to form a thin paste before adding to the pot.)

- When sauce bubbles, and ½ cup of warm water and keep stirring until water is absorbed.

- Add mastekakeya kimem.

- Add ½ cup of warm water.

- Add ½ tablespoon garlic/ginger paste.

- Add the saved butter.

- Add salt to your taste preference.

- When the sauce is a medium thickness, lower heat to simmer and continue to simmer until the butter rises to the surface.

- Sprinkle cardamom and remove from heat.

Serves 4 to 6 people

3

SPICY BEEF BRISKET DISH
Yemekerem Wot

INGREDIENTS

- 175 grams (6.2 oz.) dried minced shallots
- 350 grams (12.3 oz.) clarified butter
- 100 grams (3.5 oz.) Berbere paste
- 670 grams (1 lb. 5 oz.) beef brisket
- 1 teaspoon cardamom
- 1 teaspoon mastekakeya kimem (spice)
- ½ teaspoon fenugreek
- 2 cups of tej (Ethiopian honey wine)
- 2 cups of water
- Cinnamon
- Clove powder (according to taste)
- Salt (according to taste)

PREPARATION

- Wash meat with cold water and drain.
- Cut meat in zigzag form (across the grain) into pieces about 4 inches long.
- Mix tej and water to get 4 cups.

COOKING

- Place a heavy pot in a medium heat.
- Add the meat and stir until its juices evaporate.
- In another heavy pot, cook the fenugreek on medium heat and stir until it browns, being careful not to burn it.
- If it begins to burn, add a splash of water to deglaze it and continue to stir.
- Add ½ cup of the tej and water mixture and stir.
- Add the butter and stir until a good aroma arises.
- Add the Berbere paste and stir until the tej-water mixture is almost absorbed.
- Add another ¼ cup of the tej-water mixture and stir until it is nearly absorbed; repeat this process four times.
- Keep stirring until the Berbere sauce becomes mild.
- Taste the sauce. If it is still hot (spicy), add ¼ cup of water and continue to stir until it becomes mild.
- When the sauce is mild add the cinnamon and the clove powder as well as the meat, and stir.
- Add the rest of the tej and water mixture, stirring until the meat becomes tender.
- Add salt.
- When the butter resurfaces, sprinkle the cardamom and remove the pot from the stove and serve.
- Or, place the pot in a cool area.
- When the wot has cooled, place it into a container and put in the freezer. This dish can be preserved for a long time.

Serves 4 to 6 people

SPICY BEEF DISH, TYPE I
Yebere Zegen Wot

Note: This recipe requires marinating three ingredients three days ahead of time.

INGREDIENTS

- 500 grams (1 lb. 1 oz.) beef hind shank or brisket
- 250 grams (8.8 oz.) clarified butter
- 150 grams (5.3 oz.) Berbere paste
- 1 fresh branch Ethiopian sacred (holy) basil
- 15 grams (1 tablespoon) nech shero
- 1 teaspoon masktekakeya kimem (spice)
- ½ teaspoon koulet kimem (spice)
- ½ teaspoon fenugreek
- 1 teaspoon cardamom
- ½ bulb minced garlic (about 1 teaspoon)
- 2 tablespoons garlic/ginger paste
- Salt (according to taste)
- 5 ½ cups water

SHIRO PREPARATION

- Mix nech shiro with water to make a thin paste.

MARINATING

- Mix and keep the following ingredients in a tight container for 3 days. No refrigeration is needed.
    - Minced shallot
    - ½ bulb minced garlic
    - 1 ½ cups of water
- On the third day, strain and save the broth in a container.

MEAT BROTH PREPARATION

- Wash meat in cold water and strain.
- Boil 4 cups of water in a pot and add meat.
- Remove all particles of meat that float to the surface until broth is clear.
- Strain slowly and save broth in a container.
- Do not use any meat parts that have stuck to the bottom of the pot.
- Rinse boiled meat with cold water.
- Cut meat into small cubes.

COOKING

- Place a heavy pot on medium heat.
- Add the marinated ingredients.
- Cover with lid until steam comes out.
- Remove lid and sauté until shallots turn brownish.
- If shallots stick to the bottom of the pot, add a splash of water and stir to free them.
- Mix shallots and keep sautéing for 20 minutes until they turn brown.
- Push shallots to the edges of the pot and add fenugreek at the center.
- Sauté fenugreek until it turns brown.
- Mix with shallots.
- Add Berbere paste and sauté for 20 minutes.

RECIPE CONTINUED ▶

- Sauté until Berbere turns dark in color.
- If Berbere paste sticks to pot, splash water and continue to sauté.
- Add ¼ cup of water and sauté until liquid is nearly absorbed.
- Taste sauce to find out if Berbere paste is too hot or has become milder; if it is too hot, add ¼ cup of broth and sauté until liquid is almost absorbed.
- Add butter and sauté, saving 1 tablespoon of butter for later use.
- Sauté until a good aroma arises.
- Add meat cut into cubes, stirring until it is well coated with sauce.
- Add half of the garlic/ginger paste and keep stirring.
- Add 1 cup of broth.
- Add shiro paste, stirring constantly so it does not stick to pot.
- Add koulet kimem.
- Add 1 cup of broth and cook, stirring occasionally.
- Add mastekakeya kimem.
- Lower heat and add another ½ cup of broth.
- Let sauce bubble.
- Add the remaining garlic/ginger paste.
- Cook until sauce thickens.
- Add the remaining broth and let the sauce bubble for 10 minutes, stirring occasionally.
- Add the reserved butter.
- Taste to determine if meat is tender; if it is not, add ¼ cup of water and cook a few minutes longer.
- When meat is tender, lower heat to simmer.
- Let butter surface.
- Sprinkle cardamom and remove from heat.

Serves 4 to 6 people

5

SPICY BEEF DISH, TYPE II
Yebere Zegen Wot

INGREDIENTS

- 500 grams (1 lb. 1 oz.) beef hind shank or brisket
- 1 tablespoon shenkourt makulaya (spice)
- 200 grams (7 oz.) finely minced shallots
- 1 teaspoon koulet kimem (spice)
- 1 teaspoon mastekakeya kimem (spice)
- 100 grams (3.5 oz.) Berbere paste
- 15 grams (1 tablespoon) nech shiro
- 1 ¼ tablespoon garlic/ginger paste
- 1 teaspoon cardamom
- ¼ teaspoon fenugreek
- 1 tablespoon finely minced garlic (additional)
- 1 tablespoon finely minced ginger (additional)
- 1 ¾ cup water
- Salt (to taste)

PREPARATION

- Wash meat and strain.
- Dice meat into small cubes.
- Mix shiro with water to make a thin paste.

RECIPE CONTINUED ▶

COOKING

- Place heavy pot on medium heat.

- Add the shallots and garlic.

- Cover with lid until steam comes out.

- If shallots stick to pot while sautéing, push the free shallots away from the sticking area and splash water where the shallots are sticking, then scrape and mix with the other shallots.

- Mix shallots and keep sautéing until shallots turn brown.

- Push shallots to the edges of the pot and add fenugreek in the center.

- Sauté the fenugreek until it turns brown, then mix with shallots.

- Add cubed meat cut to pot and cover with lid.

- The meat will release liquid as it cooks.

- Remove lid and sauté until liquid is absorbed.

- Add butter and sauté, saving 1 tablespoon of butter for later use.

- Add ½ tablespoon garlic/ginger paste and stir for about two minutes

- Add Berbere paste and sauté for 20 minutes until Berbere turns dark in color.

- If Berbere paste sticks to pot, splash water to release it and keep on sautéing.

- Add ¼ cup of water and sauté until liquid is nearly absorbed.

- Add mastekakeya kimem and stir for two minutes.

- Add ¼ cup of water and stir until liquid is almost absorbed.

- Repeat this procedure one more time.

- Taste the sauce to determine if Berbere paste is too hot or mild; if it is too hot, add ¼ cup of water and cook a while longer.

- When Berbere paste has become milder, add the remaining garlic/ginger past and stir.

- Add ½ cup of water and lower heat.

- Let the sauce bubble and cook for 10 minutes while stirring occasionally.

- When sauce thickens add the reserved 1 tablespoon butter.

- Add salt.

- Add ½ cup water and cook the sauce until thickens.

- Taste the meat for tenderness; if it is not done, keep cooking and add a little amount of water.

- When meat becomes tender, lower heat to simmer.

- Cook until butter surfaces.

- Sprinkle cardamom and remove from heat.

Serves 4 to 6 people

6

SPICY BEEF HUMP DISH

Yesega Bozena Shiro with Beef Hump

INGREDIENTS

- 50 grams (1.8 oz.) minced shallots
- 150 grams (5.3 oz.) clarified butter
- 250 grams (8.8 oz.) lean beef meat
- 200 grams (7 oz.) beef hump
- 200 grams (7 oz) mitin shiro powder
- salt (to taste)

PREPARATION

- Wash all meat in cold water.
- Dice lean meat into bite-sized cubes.
- Dice hump meat into bite-sized cubes.

BROTH PREPARATION

- Add water in a pot and heat until warm.
- Add 150 grams (5.3 oz.) beef meat and heat.
- Remove all particles and fat that floats to the top with a spatula; keep removing it until broth is clear.
- Add all of the shallots.
- Boil for 30 minutes.
- Remove pot from stove and let stand for 15 minutes.
- Save the broth in a bowl.

COOKING

- Place a heavy pot on medium high heat.
- Add the broth and heat until almost boiling.
- Add half of the clarified butter and boil for a few minutes.
- Mix the mitin shiro powder with cold water to create a paste that is not too thick.
- Add mitin shiro paste to the pot and continuously stir to keep lumps from forming
- Continue stirring to keep the shiro from sticking to the bottom of the pot; if it sticks to the bottom, add a splash of water to make it loose enough to stir.
- Cook this sauce for 25 minutes on medium heat, stirring occasionally.
- Add the meats and consistently stir for about five minutes, or until the meat is cooked.
- Add the rest of the butter and cook until it surfaces from the shiro sauce.
- Once the butter surfaces, remove from heat; do not cook shiro for a long time after adding the meat because it will make the meat dry and tough.
- When the meat is ready, serve with injera.

Serves 4 to 6 people

RECIPE CONTINUED ▶

7

SPICY BEEF HUMP WITH SHIRO DISH
Yeshagna Bozena Shiro

INGREDIENTS

- 50 grams (1.8 oz.) minced shallots
- 150 grams (5.3 oz.) clarified butter
- 250 grams (8.8 oz.) lean beef
- 200 grams (7 oz.) oxen hump
- 200 grams (7 oz.) of nech shiro powder
- Salt (to taste)

PREPARATION

- Wash all meat in cold water.
- Dice lean meat into bite-sized cubes.
- Dice hump meat into bite-sized cubes.

BROTH PREPARATION

- Add water in a pot and heat until warm.
- Add 150 grams (5.3 oz.) beef and heat.
- With a rubber scraper, remove all particles and fat that floats to the top; keep removing it until broth is clear.
- Add all of the shallots.
- Boil for 30 minutes.
- Remove pot from stove and let stand for 15 minutes.
- Save the broth in a bowl.

COOKING

- Place a heavy pot on medium high heat.
- Add the broth and heat until almost boiling.
- Add 125 grams (4.4 oz.) clarified butter and boil for a few minutes.
- Mix the shiro powder with cold water to create a paste that is not too thick.
- Add the shiro paste to the pot and continuously stir to keep lumps from forming.
- Continue stirring to keep the shiro from sticking to the bottom of the pot; if it sticks to the bottom, add a splash of water to make it loose enough to stir.
- Cook this sauce for 25 minutes on medium heat, stirring occasionally.
- Add the meats and continue stirring for about five minutes, or until the meat is cooked.
- Add 1 tablespoon of butter and cook until the butter surfaces from the shiro sauce.
- Once the butter surfaces, remove from heat; do not cook shiro for a long time after adding the meat because it will make the meat dry and tough.
- When the meat is ready, serve with injera.

Serves 4 to 6 people

SPICY BEEF JERKY DISH
Yezelbo Quanta Wot

INGREDIENTS

- 275 grams (9.7 oz.) quanta (Ethiopian beef jerky)
- 1 teaspoon koulet kimem (spice)
- 250 grams (8.8 oz.) finely minced shallots
- 1 teaspoon mastekakeya kimem (spice)
- 200 grams (7 oz.) clarified butter
- 90 grams (3.2 oz.) Berbere paste
- 20 grams (1 ⅓ tablespoons) nech shiro
- 1 level teaspoon fenugreek
- 1 teaspoon cardamom
- 1 tablespoon garlic/ginger paste
- 2 ¼ cups water
- salt (to taste)

PREPARATION

- Cut quanta into 5 cm. (2 in.) pieces
- Wash quanta.
- Mix nech shiro with 1 cup cold water.

COOKING

- Place a heavy pot on medium heat.
- Add shallots.
- Cover with lid until steam starts to come out.
- Remove lid and sauté for 20 minutes until shallots wilt and turn brownish.
- If shallots stick to bottom of the pot, push the loose shallots toward the edge of pot and add a splash of water.
- Mix shallots and sauté until color is brownish.
- Move shallots to the edges of pot to free the center.
- Add fenugreek and sauté until it turns brown.
- If fenugreek becomes too brown, add a splash of water.
- Add butter and sauté for 15 minutes; saving 1 tablespoon of butter for later use.
- When a good aroma rises, add ginger/garlic paste and stir continuously.
- Add Berbere paste and sauté for 20 minutes.
- Add koulet kimem.
- Continue to stir until Berbere paste gets dark in color.
- Add ¼ cup water and sauté until water is nearly absorbed.
- Repeat the process one more time.
- Taste sauce to find out if Berbere paste is too hot or has become milder; if it is too hot, add ¼ cup of broth and sauté until liquid is almost absorbed.

RECIPE CONTINUED ▶

- Add quanta.

- Sauté for about 15 minutes.

- Pour in the nech shiro mixture.

- Stir constantly so shiro does not stick to pot.

- Cook for 15 minutes.

- When a good aroma rises, add ½ cup water and salt.

- Stir and cook until sauce thickens for about 10 minutes.

- Add mastekakeya kimem

- Add butter that was set aside.

- When sauces thickens, add another ½ cup of water.

- Lower heat a little and let the wot bubble for 10 minutes.

- Taste to determine if quanta is tender; if it is not tender add another ½ cup of water and cook a bit longer.

- When quanta is ready, lower heat to simmer, stirring occasionally until butter surfaces.

- Sprinkle cardamom and remove from heat.

Serves 4 to 6 people

SPICY CHICKEN DISH, TYPE 1
Yedoro Wot

INGREDIENTS

- 1 whole chicken

- 1 lime or lemon

- 1 teaspoon mastekakeya kimem (spice)

- 12 hard boiled eggs, shells removed

- 350 grams (12.3 oz.) finely minced shallots

- 1 teaspoon cardamom

- 300 grams (10.6 oz.) clarified butter

- 100 grams (3.5 oz.) Berbere paste

- 2 ½ cups of warm water

- 1 tablespoon garlic/ginger paste

- salt (to taste)

CHICKEN PREPARATION

- Skin the chicken and cut it into pieces (see photo).

- Scrape off yellow fatty substance with knife and dispose.

- Place cold water in a large container.

- Cut a lime/lemon into pieces and place into container.

- Wash the chicken several times in the cold water until the meat is odorless.

- Place chicken on sieve and remove lime/lemon pieces.

- Squeeze out water from chicken parts before placing in cooking pot.

RECIPE CONTINUED ▶

COOKING

- Place a heavy pot on medium heat.

- Put in the shallots in the pot and cover.

- Remove the lid when steam rises and begin to stir.

- Sauté shallots for 30 minutes. If shallots stick to pot while sautéing, push the free shallots away and splash water where the shallots are sticking, then scrape and mix with the other shallots.

- Mix the shallots and continue to sauté until they becomes brownish.

- Add butter and sauté for 15 minutes, reserving 1 tablespoon of butter for later use.

- Add ¼ cup warm water.

- Add ½ tablespoon of the garlic/ginger paste.

- Constantly stir while cooking.

- When sauce bubbles, add the Berbere paste.

- Stir until water is nearly absorbed.

- Add ¼ cup warm water.

- Add the remaining garlic/ginger paste.

- Add ¼ cup warm water and keep stirring until water is nearly absorbed.

- Repeat this process three times.

- Sautéing the Berbere paste will take 20 to 25 minutes.

- Taste sauce to find out if Berbere paste is too hot or has become milder; if it is too hot, add ¼ cup of broth and sauté until liquid is almost absorbed.

- When sauce is milder and darker in color, add the chicken parts.

- Add the saved 1 tablespoon butter and continue stirring until chicken meat is almost fried.

- Add ½ cup warm water.

- Cook until water is almost absorbed and sauce is thickened.

- Add another ½ cup of warm water and stir occasionally while cooking, until sauce is thick.

- Check to determine if the meat is tender.

- When meat is done, add the cardamom.

- Add the whole eggs and cook for 2 minutes.

- Add salt.

- Lower heat to simmer until butter surfaces.

- Remove from heat.

Serves 4 to 6 people

RECIPE CONTINUED ▶

TRADITIONAL ETHIOPIAN COOKBOOK

10

SPICY CHICKEN DISH WITH TEJ, TYPE II
Doro Wot with Tej

INGREDIENTS

- 1 whole chicken
- 1 lime or lemon
- 12 hard boiled eggs, shells removed
- 350 grams (12.3 oz.) finely minced shallots
- 1 teaspoon mastekakeya kimem (spice)
- 1 teaspoon cardamom
- 300 grams (10.6 oz.) clarified butter
- 100 grams (3.5 oz.) Berbere paste
- 1 tablespoon garlic/ginger paste
- salt (to taste)
- 1 cup cold water
- 1 cup warm water
- 1 cup dry tej (Ethiopian honey wine)

CHICKEN PREPARATION

- Skin chicken and cut it into pieces (see photo).
- Scrape off yellow fatty substance with knife and dispose.
- Wash several times in a container with cut lime or lemon pieces and cold water until chicken is odorless.
- Place chicken pieces on a sieve.
- Squeeze out water from chicken pieces before putting in cooking pot.

TEJ PREPARATION

- Mix ¼ cup tej with garlic/ginger paste.
- Mix ¾ cup tej with 1 cup of cold water.

COOKING

- Place a heavy pot on medium heat.
- Put in the shallots in the pot and cover.
- Remove lid when steam rises and stir to keep shallots from sticking. If shallots stick to pot while sautéing, push the free shallots away and splash water where the shallots are sticking, then scrape and mix with the other shallots.
- When juice from the shallots has evaporated, add butter, reserving 1 tablespoon for later use.
- Stir constantly.
- Sauté until shallots are brownish in color.

RECIPE CONTINUED ▶

- When a good aroma rises, add the mixture of tej and garlic/ginger paste, stirring until a good aroma rises.

- Add Berbere paste and continue stirring until the color of the Berbere paste becomes darker.

- Add ¼ cup of tej and cold water mixture and cook, stirring until water is absorbed.

- Repeat the same process three times.

- Add the chicken parts and keep stirring.

- When meat is approximately half done, add ¼ cup of tej and garlic/ginger paste.

- Add the reserved 1 tablespoon butter.

- Add the mastekakeya kimem.

- Let the sauce bubble.

- When sauce starts to thicken, add ½ cup warm water and stir while cooking a few minutes longer.

- Add the remaining ½ cup of warm water and mix well.

- Add the cardamom.

- Add the whole eggs and cook for 2 minutes.

- Add salt.

- Reduce heat to simmer and cook until butter surfaces.

- Remove from heat.

Serves 4 to 6 people

11

SPICY FISH DISH
Fers Assa Wot

INGREDIENTS

- 400 grams (14 oz.) of any white-meat fish
- ¼ teaspoon black pepper
- 350 grams (12.3 oz.) finely minced shallots
- 1/8 teaspoon cumin
- ¾ cup oil
- 100 grams (3.5 oz.) Berbere paste
- 1 tablespoon garlic/ginger paste
- ½ teaspoon koulet kimem (spice)
- 1 teaspoon cardamom
- ½ cup water
- ½ cup tej (Ethiopian honey wine)
- salt (to taste)

PREPARATION

- Clean fish and cut into large pieces.
- Mix ¼ cup tej with garlic/ginger paste.
- Mix ¼ cup tej with water.

COOKING

- Place heavy pot on medium heat.
- Put shallots in the pot and cover with lid.
- Remove lid when steam starts to come out.
- Sauté shallots until they become brownish.

- If shallots stick to pot while sautéing, push the free shallots away and splash water where the shallots are sticking, then scrape and mix with the other shallots.
- Add oil and sauté for 10 minutes.
- Add tej and garlic/ginger mixture and stir.
- Add Berbere paste and sauté for 20 minutes until it darkens in color.
- If Berbere paste sticks to bottom of pot, add ⅛ cup of water
- Add koulet kimem.
- Add ¼ cup of tej and water mixture and stir.
- Repeat the same process until tej and water mixture is all used
- Taste to determine if Berbere paste is still too hot or mild, if too hot add ¼ cup of water and cook a few minutes more.
- When sauce is milder, add mastekakeya kimem.
- Cook and stir occasionally until sauce thickens.
- Add fish and cook, stirring occasionally and slowly. Fish is cooked when it begins to flake apart.
- Add ¼ cup of water and cook until sauce thickens again.
- Lower heat to simmer and let oil surface.
- Add salt.
- Sprinkle cardamom and cumin.
- Remove from heat.

Serves 4 to 6 people

12

SPICY FISH JERKY DISH
Fers Assa Wot

INGREDIENTS

- 175 grams (6.2 oz.) fish jerky (quanta, any kind)
- ¾ cup cooking oil
- 235 grams (8.3 oz.) finely minced shallots
- ¼ teaspoon fenugreek
- 100 grams (3.5 oz.) Berbere paste
- 1 teaspoon cardamom
- 30 grams (2 tablespoons) flaxseed
- 1 ½ cups warm water
- 1 tablespoon garlic/ginger paste
- salt (to taste)

PREPARATION

- Cut quanta into small pieces.
- Wash quanta with cold water and strain.
- Mix the garlic/ginger paste and flaxseed.

COOKING

- Place a heavy pot on medium heat.
- Add shallots and cover with lid.
- Remove lid when steam starts to escape.
- Sauté for about 20 minutes until shallots wilt and turn brownish.

- If shallots stick to pot while sautéing, push the free shallots away and splash water where the shallots are sticking, then scrape and mix with the other shallots.
- Add oil and sauté for 10 minutes until a good aroma rises.
- Add garlic/ginger paste and flaxseed mixture.
- Add Berbere paste and sauté for 20 minutes until it gets darker in color, stirring constantly to keep it from sticking to the pot.
- If sticking occurs, sprinkle a small amount of water and continue sautéing.
- Add ½ cup warm water and cook until water is nearly completely absorbed.
- Taste sauce to find out if Berbere paste is too hot or has become milder; if it is too hot, add ¼ cup of broth and sauté until liquid is almost absorbed.
- When sauce is mild, add quanta and sauté until quanta is almost fried.
- Add ½ cup of warm water and cook until water is almost absorbed.
- Repeat the same process one more time.
- Taste if quanta is done (tender).
- If quanta is not done, add ¼ cup of warm water and cook a few minutes more.
- When quanta is ready, lower heat.
- Add salt.
- When oil surfaces, sprinkle cardamom.
- Remove from heat.

Serves 4 to 6 people

13

SPICY LAMB HIND LEG DISH
Enfelay Wot

INGREDIENTS

- 1 lamb hind leg
- 1 tablespoon garlic/ginger paste
- 600 grams (1 lb. 5 oz.) lamb meat with bones
- 300 grams (10.6 oz.) minced shallots
- 300 grams (10.6 oz.) clarified butter
- 170 grams (6 oz.) awaze mixed with tej (see preparation instructions below)
- Up to 4 cups warm water
- 1 ¾ cups tej (Ethiopian honey wine)
- 2 teaspoons black pepper
- ¼ teaspoon cumin
- 1 teaspoon salt

AWAZE PREPARATION

- Mix the awaze with 1 ½ cups tej to make a paste.

MEAT BROTH PREPARATION

- Rinse the meat and bone with cold water and strain.
- Place a tall pot on medium high heat.
- Put meat and bone in pot.
- Sauté meat and bone until meat juice coming out is almost evaporated.
- Add shallots and sauté until they wilt.

- Add 200 grams (7 oz.) butter and sauté for 10 minutes.
- Add garlic/ginger paste.
- When a good aroma arises, add 2 cups of warm water and boil.
- Add ¼ cup tej as the water boils.
- Add 1 cup of warm water and keep boiling.
- Add cumin.
- Add 2 cups of warm water and keep boiling.
- Check meat to determine when it is approximately half done.
- When meat is half done, add awaze-tej paste.
- Keep boiling until meat is tender.
- When meat is done, strain the broth.
- Discard meat and bones.

RECIPE CONTINUED ▶

LAMB HIND LEG PREPARATION

- Make a slit from the knee down the thigh of the hind leg.

- Remove the femur.

- Meat that was attached to femur will hang loose; cut any hanging meat vertically, starting from the knee.

- The width of each piece should be about 3 inches.

- Cut each piece in zigzag fashion.

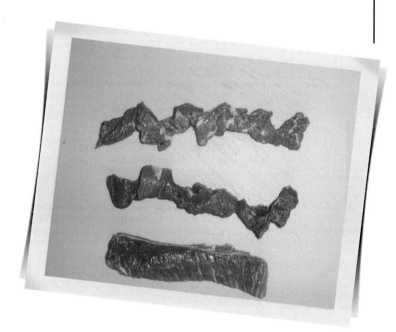

LAMB LEG

- Place leg on cutting board.

- Rub salt and black pepper on lamb leg.

- Warm the broth.

- Immerse the lamb leg in the broth, covering all parts.

- Keep in broth until the meat's color becomes light brown.

- Remove meat from broth and place on serving dish.

- In another serving dish, place small pieces of injera.

- Pour broth on injera and serve both dishes together.

Serves 4 to 6 people

14

SPICY LAMB SHANK DISH
Yebeg tibs wot

INGREDIENTS

- 350 grams (12.3 oz.) finely minced shallots
- 300 grams (10.6 oz.) clarified butter
- 100 grams (3.5 oz.) Berbere paste
- 700 grams (1 lb. 9 oz.) lamb hind shank cut in cubes
- 1 tablespoon garlic /ginger paste
- 1 teaspoon cardamom
- 1 teaspoon of mastekakeya kimem (spice)
- 1 tablespoon garlic ginger paste
- 1 ¾ cup dry tej (Ethiopian honey wine)
- 1 ½ cup of warm water

PREPARATION

- Wash meat thoroughly with cold water and strain.
- Mix 1 ½ cup of tej with 1 cup of water.
- Mix ¼ cup of tej with 1 tablespoon of garlic/ ginger paste.

COOKING

- Place a heavy pot on a medium heat.
- Add minced shallots and cover pan.
- Remove the lid once the steam begins to escape.

- Stir the shallots for 20 minutes. Use 1 ¼ cup of water to deglaze the shallots as they stick to the bottom of the pot and continue to stir until they brown.
- Save 1 tablespoon of the butter to be used later before adding the remainder.
- Add the clarified butter to the shallots and sauté for 10 minutes.
- Add ½ tablespoon of the tej and garlic ginger mixture and sauté and keep stirring for a few minutes.
- Add the Berbere paste and sauté by stirring for 20 minutes until the Berbere becomes darker in color.
- Add ¼ cup of tej and water mixture and stir until it is absorbed.
- Repeat this process two more times.
- Taste to see if the sauce is hot (spicy). If it is, add ¼ cup of warm water and stir until the sauce becomes mild.
- Add meat when the liquid is almost fully absorbed and continue to stir until the meat is almost fully cooked.
- Add ½ cup of the tej-water mixture and stir until the mixture is almost absorbed. Repeat the process until the mixture is used.
- Add the rest of the garlic ginger and tej mixture until mixture is used.
- Add the 1 tablespoon of butter that was put aside; stir until meat is fully cooked.
- Add ½ cup of warm water and cook until sauce thickens.
- When sauce has thickened and has reached the desired consistency, lower heat and simmer until the butter surfaces.
- Add cardamom and remove the pot from heat.
- Taste the meat; when meat is tender, the wot is ready.
- Remove from heat.

Serves 4 to 6 people.

GRAIN DISHES

1

BERBERE SHIRO DISH
Yebeten Berbere Shiro Wot

INGREDIENTS

- 4 cups water
- 4 tablespoons cooking oil
- One small branch Ethiopian holy basil
- ½ teaspoon Berbere powder
- 3 tablespoon nech shiro
- salt (to taste)
- prepared Injera

NECH SHIRO PREPARATION

- Mix nech shiro in a bowl with water to make a thin paste.

COOKING

- Place a heavy pot on high heat.
- Add the water and bring to a boil.
- Lower heat to medium high.
- Add 1 tablespoon oil.
- Add Berbere powder and stir constantly so it does not overflow.
- When mixture is about to bubble, add the shiro paste.
- Stir occasionally as it cooks.
- Add the remaining oil.
- Add the fresh basil.
- Let it bubble for about 5 minutes.
- Add salt.
- Cook for 45 minutes on medium heat, then lower heat to simmer.
- When oil surfaces, remove from heat.

Serves 4 to 6 people

2

SPICY DISH WITH INJERA
Yetom Wot Gefelfel

INGREDIENTS

- 100 grams (3.5 oz.) Berbere paste
- 1 teaspoon cardamom
- 300 grams (10.6 oz.) finely minced shallots
- 1 tablespoon garlic/ginger paste
- 1 ½ tablespoon shiro for spicy dish (see Glossary)
- ¾ cup cooking oil
- 3 cups warm water
- 1 teaspoon mastekakeya kimem (spice)
- 1 teaspoon koulet kimem (spice)
- pinch of fenugreek
- salt (to taste)
- prepared Injera

SHERO PREPARATION

- Mix shiro with water to make a thin paste.

COOKING

- Place a heavy pot on medium heat.
- Add shallots and cover with lid.
- Remove lid when steam starts to come out and begin to stir.
- Sauté the shallots until they wilt and become brownish, about 15 minutes.

- If shallots stick to pot while sautéing, push the free shallots away from the sticking area and splash water where the shallots are sticking, then scrape and mix with the other shallots.
- Continue to sauté until shallots begin to turn brown.
- Add fenugreek to the center of the pot and sauté until it becomes brown in color.
- Mix with shallots.
- Add oil and sauté for about 10 minutes.
- Add garlic/ginger paste and sauté for 5 minutes until a good aroma rises.
- Add Berbere paste and sauté for about 20 minutes until the paste darkens.
- Add ¼ cup of warm water and cook for 10 minutes until sauce thickens.
- Add shiro paste and stir constantly until shiro thickens.
- Add ¼ cup of water and stir continuously.
- Repeat the same process until all 2 cups of water are used and the Berbere sauce becomes mild when tasted.
- If Berbere sauce is still too hot, add ¼ cup of warm water and cook a while longer.
- When Berbere sauce becomes mild, add koulet kimem and salt and cook for 5 minutes.
- Add mastekakeya kimem and cook for 5 minutes.
- Add 1 cup warm water and the remaining garlic/ginger paste.
- Lower the heat and let the sauce bubble for about 10 minutes until the spices blend well with the sauce.
- Lower heat to simmer and continue to cook, stirring slowly and occasionally.
- When oil surfaces, sprinkle the mixture with cardamom and remove from heat.
- Place small pieces of injera onto a serving plate.
- Pour sauce over injera and slowly mix well.

Serves 4 to 6 people

3

SPICY DOYO DISH
Yemasero Doyo Wot

INGREDIENTS

- 60 grams (2.1 oz.) nech shiro
- 50 grams (1.8 oz.) finely minced shallots
- 20 grams (1 tablespoon) Berbere powder
- ½ leveled teaspoon fenugreek
- 3 cups water
- 2 tablespoon cooking oil
- salt (to taste)
- prepared Injera

NECH SHIRO PREPARATION

- Mix nech shiro with water in a bowl to make a thin paste.

COOKING

- Place a heavy pot (preferably a clay pot) on medium heat.
- When the pot gets warm, add fenugreek and stir until it gets dark brown.
- Add shallots and sauté until a good aroma rises.
- Add 2 cups water and let it bubble for about 10 minutes.
- Add Berbere powder, and let it boil for about 10 minutes.
- Add nech shiro paste and cook until it bubbles.
- Add oil and salt.

- Add 1 cup of water and keep on cooking while stirring occasionally.
- Cook for 40 minutes, lowering heat to simmer.
- When oil surfaces, remove from heat.
- Sauce should not be very thick.

Serves 4 to 6 people

SPICY GARBANZO FLOUR DISH
Yeshimbra Assa Wot

INGREDIENTS

- 150 grams (5.3 oz.) garbanzo flour
- 1 level teaspoon kishin kimem (spice – see Glossary)
- 1 teaspoon mastekakeya kimem (spice)
- 250 grams (8.8 oz.) finely minced shallots
- 100 grams (3.5 oz.) Berbere paste
- 1 tablespoon garlic/ginger paste
- 1 teaspoon cardamom
- ½ teaspoon fenugreek
- 5 tablespoons cooking oil
- ¾ cups cooking oil
- 2 3/4 cups of water
- salt (to taste)

SHIMBRA FLOUR PREPARATION

- Mix garbanzo flour with salt.
- Add 1 tablespoon oil and knead.
- Add ¼ cup cold water and continue to knead.
- Roll out the dough to about a 1-inch thickness.
- Use a fish-shaped cookie cutter to cut dough into shapes.

FRYING

- Place frying pan on high heat.
- Add ¼ cup cooking oil.
- When oil bubbles, add fish shaped dough pieces and fry the first side until golden.
- Flip and fry the second side until golden.
- Place into a container.

COOKING

- Place a heavy pot on medium heat.
- Add shallots and cover with lid.
- Remove the lid when steam starts to escape.
- Sauté for about 20 minutes until shallots wilt and turn brownish.
- If shallots stick to the pot while sautéing, push the free shallots away and add a splash water where shallots are sticking. Then, mix with the rest of shallot and sauté.
- When shallots are brownish, move shallots to the edges of the pot.
- Place fenugreek at center of pot and sauté until it is brown, then mix with the shallots.
- Add the oil and sauté for about 10 minutes until a good aroma arises.
- Add kishin kimem and cook for about 5 minutes.
- Add ½ tablespoon garlic/ginger paste.

RECIPE CONTINUED ▶

- Add Berbere paste and sauté for 20 minutes until it gets darker in color, stirring constantly so it does not stick to pot; if sauce sticks to pot, add a splash of water and continue sautéing.

- Add ¼ cup of warm water and cook until water is almost absorbed.

- Taste sauce to find out if Berbere sauce is too hot or has become milder.

- If sauce is still too hot, add ¼ cup of warm water and sauté.

- Add the remaining garlic/ginger paste and stir for about 3 minutes.

- Add ¼ cup of warm water and stir for about 10 minutes until sauce thickens.

- Repeat the same process three times.

- Taste sauce to find out if Berbere is still too hot or has become mild; if sauce is still too hot, add ¼ cup of warm water and cook a while longer.

- If sauce has become mild, add mastekakeya kimem.

- Lower heat and cook until sauce thickens, for about 15 minutes.

- Add the garbanzo dough cut into fish shapes (shimbera assa) and cook for 10 minutes.

- Lower to simmer and cook until oil surfaces.

- Add salt.

- Sprinkle cardamom and remove from heat.

Serves 4 to 6 people

5

SPICY GARBANZO SPLIT PEA DISH

Yeshimbra Kik
Merek Wot

INGREDIENTS

- 150 grams (5.3 oz.) garbanzo split peas
- 230 grams (8.1 oz.) finely minced shallots
- 100 grams (3.5 oz.) Berbere paste
- ¾ cup cooking oil
- 1 tablespoon garlic/ginger paste
- 1 teaspoon cardamom
- 3 cups water
- salt (to taste)

SPLIT GARBANZO PEAS PREPARATION

- Wash split garbanzo peas thoroughly with cold water and strain.
- Boil 3 cups of water.
- Add the split garbanzo peas and cook until they are half done.
- Strain and save the water for later use.

COOKING

- Place a heavy pot on medium heat.
- Add shallots and cover with lid.
- Remove lid when steam starts to come out and begin to stir.
- Sauté the shallots until they wilt and become brownish, about 15 minutes.

- When shallots stick to pot, move free shallots to the edge of pot and add a splash of water and stir to free shallots, then mix with the rest of shallots and continue to sauté until shallots turn brownish.
- Push shallots toward the edges of the pot and add fenugreek to center of the pot. Sauté until it becomes brown in color, then mix with shallots.
- Add oil and sauté for about 10 minutes.
- Add ½ tablespoon garlic/ginger paste and sauté for 5 minutes until a good aroma rises.
- Add Berbere paste and sauté for about 20 minutes until the paste gets dark in color.
- Add ½ cup of the water used to boil the chick peas and cook until liquid is almost absorbed.
- Add ¼ cup of same water and cook, stirring until liquid is almost absorbed.
- Repeat the process one more time.
- Taste the sauce to find out if the Berbere sauce has become mild or not. If not, add ¼ cup of warm water and sauté.
- When Berbere sauce gets mild, add the garbanzo split peas and sauté for about 10 minutes until a good aroma rises.
- When a good aroma rises, add ½ cup of saved water and cook until sauce becomes thicker.
- Add the remaining garlic/ginger paste and cook for 3 minutes.
- Add 1 cup of saved water and let the sauce bubble until it gets thicker, making sure that the sauce doesn't become too thick.
- Lower heat and sprinkle cardamom.
- Add salt.
- Simmer until oil surfaces and remove from heat.

Serves 4 to 6 people

6

SPICY RED LENTILS DISH
Yedifin Messer Wot

INGREDIENTS

- 215 grams (7.6 oz.) whole red lentils
- 250 grams (8.8 oz.) finely minced shallots
- 100 grams (3.5 oz.) Berbere paste
- 1 tablespoon garlic/ginger paste
- ½ teaspoon koulet kimem (spice)
- 1 tablespoon mastekakeya kimem (spice)
- 1 pinch fenugreek
- 1 teaspoon cardamom
- 4 ¾ cups water
- ¾ cup cooking oil
- salt (to taste)

LENTIL PREPARATION

- Wash lentils in cold water and strain.
- Place pot on high heat and add three cups of water.
- When water boils, add lentils.
- Cook for three minutes or until half done.
- Strain and save the water for later use.

COOKING

- Add shallots to the pan and cover with a lid.
- Remove lid when steam starts to escape.
- Sauté for about 20 minutes until shallots wilt and turn brownish.
- If shallots stick to pot while sautéing, push the free shallot away and splash water where the shallots are sticking. Mix the freed shallots with the rest and sauté.
- When shallots are brownish, move shallots to the edges of the pot.
- Place fenugreek in the center of the pot and sauté until brown.
- Mix fenugreek with the shallots and sauté for 1 minute.
- Add cooking oil and sauté for about 10 minutes or until a good aroma rises.
- Add ½ tablespoon garlic/ginger paste.
- Sauté for about three minutes.
- Add Berbere paste and sauté until it gets dark in color or for about 20 minutes.
- Add ¼ cup warm water and stir until water is almost absorbed.
- Add koulet kimem.

RECIPE CONTINUED ▶

- Repeat the process of adding ¼ cup of warm water three times.
- When liquid is almost absorbed, taste the sauce to find out if the Berbere paste is hot or mild; if sauce is still too hot, add ¼ cup of warm water and cook a while longer.
- When sauce is mild, add lentils and cook until a good aroma rises (about 10 minutes).
- Add mastekakeya kimem.
- Add ¼ cup of reserved water used to boil lentils.
- Repeat the same process until lentils are tender.
- Add the rest of garlic/ginger paste and cook for 5 minutes.
- Add salt.
- Lower heat to simmer and cook until oil surfaces.
- Sprinkle cardamom and remove from heat.

Serves 4 to 6 people.

7

SPICY SPLIT PEA DISH
Ye ater wochet abish wot

INGREDIENTS

- 200 grams (7 oz.) ater (yellow split peas)
- 250 grams (8.8 oz.) finely minced shallots
- 100 grams (3.5 oz.) Berbere paste
- 1 ½ tablespoons garlic/ginger paste
- 1 tablespoon finely minced garlic
- 1 tablespoon finely minced ginger
- 1 ¼ cup cooking oil
- ½ teaspoon shenkourt kimem (spice)
- 1 level teaspoon makoulaya kimem (spice) MM will check. Instructions below call for koulet kimem
- 4 ¼ cups warm water
- 1 teaspoon and a pinch of fenugreek
- salt (to taste)

FENUGREEK BROTH PREPARATION

- Place sauce in pot on medium heat.
- Add 1 teaspoon fenugreek and stir until it becomes dark brown in color.
- Lower heat.
- Add 2 ½ cups of water and simmer for 40 minutes.
- Remove from heat and set aside for 10 minutes.
- Strain with cloth into a bowl before discarding the fenugreek remaining on the cloth.

RECIPE CONTINUED▶

INGREDIENTS

- 200 grams (7 oz.) ater (yellow split peas)
- 250 grams (8.8 oz.) finely minced shallots
- 100 grams (3.5 oz.) Berbere paste
- 1 ½ tablespoons garlic/ginger paste
- 1 tablespoon finely minced garlic
- 1 tablespoon finely minced ginger
- 1 ¼ cup cooking oil
- ½ teaspoon shenkourt kimem (spice)
- 1 level teaspoon makoulaya kimem (spice) MM will check. Instructions below call for koulet kimem
- 4 ¼ cups warm water
- 1 teaspoon and a pinch of fenugreek
- salt (to taste)

FENUGREEK BROTH PREPARATION

- Place sauce in pot on medium heat.
- Add 1 teaspoon fenugreek and stir until it becomes dark brown in color.
- Lower heat.
- Add 2 ½ cups of water and simmer for 40 minutes.
- Remove from heat and set aside for 10 minutes.
- Strain with cloth into a bowl before discarding the fenugreek remaining on the cloth.

ATER (YELLOW SPLIT PEAS) PREPARATION

- Wash split peas thoroughly with cold water and strain.
- Boil 2 ½ cups of water in a sauce pan.
- Add the split peas and cook until the peas are well done.

COOKING

- Place a heavy pot on medium heat.
- Add shallots, minced garlic, and minced ginger; cover with a lid.
- Remove lid when steam starts to escape.
- Sauté for about 20 minutes until shallots wilt and turn brownish.
- If shallots stick to pot while sautéing, push the free shallots to the edges of the pot and add ¼ cup of warm water where the shallots are sticking and stir.
- Mix with the rest of shallots and sauté.
- When shallots are brownish, move the shallots to the edges of the pot.
- Place fenugreek at center of pot and sauté until it is brown.
- Mix with the shallots and sauté for 1 minute.
- Add cooking oil and sauté for about 10 minutes or until a good aroma rises.
- Add ½ tablespoon garlic/ginger paste and the shenkourt kimem.
- Sauté for about three minutes.
- Add Berbere paste and sauté until it gets dark in color or for about 20 minutes.
- Add ¼ cup of fenugreek broth and stir until the water is almost absorbed.
- Repeat the process of adding ¼ cup of fenugreek broth three times.
- When liquid is almost absorbed, taste to find out if Berbere paste is still hot or has become milder.
- If sauce is still too hot, add ¼ cup of warm water and cook a while longer.
- When Berbere paste becomes mild and dark, add the oil.
- Let it bubble and cook for 5 minutes.

RECIPE CONTINUED ▶

- Add koulet kimem and cook for 5 minutes.

- Add mastekakeya kimem and cook for 3 minutes, stirring consistently.

- When oil surfaces, add mashed split peas.

- Add ½ cup fenugreek broth cook for about 5 minutes.

- Add the remaining garlic/ginger paste.

- Add salt.

- Cook until sauce thickens.

- Lower heat and cook, stirring occasionally.

- When oil surfaces, remove from heat.

Serves 4 to 6 people.

SPROUTED FAVA BEENS WITH AWAZE DISH

Yebakela Bekolt Awaze Alicha Merek

Note: The fava beans must be sprouted ahead of time. This can take two to three days.

INGREDIENTS

- 250 grams (8.8 oz.) sprouted fava beans

- 250 grams (8.8 oz.) minced shallots

- 35 grams (2 1/3 tablespoons) awaze

- 1 leveled tablespoon ginger/garlic paste

- 1 cup cooking oil

- ¼ cup tej (Ethiopian honey wine)

- 4 cups warm water

- Salt (to taste)

- Prepared Injera

FAVA BEAN PREPARATION

- Place fava beans in a container and cover with cold water.

- Place in a spot at room temperature.

- Wait until the beans sprout (this takes two to three days).

- Beans are ready to use when they just begin to sprout; do not let the beans sprout fully.

RECIPE CONTINUED ▶

AWAZE PREPARATION

- Mix awaze with ½ cup oil and ¼ cup tej and set aside.

COOKING

- Place a pot on medium high heat.

- Add the shallots to the pot and cover with a lid.

- When steam starts to come out, remove the lid and start to stir.

- Pour in the remaining ¼ cup cooking oil and keep stirring.

- When the mixture bubbles, add ½ tablespoon ginger/garlic paste and stir occasionally.

- When a good aroma rises, add ¼ cup warm water and lower the heat.

- When water is almost absorbed, add another ½ cup warm water and bring it to a simmer.

- Add the awaze and the fava beans.

- Cook until beans are almost done.

- Add the remaining ginger/garlic paste, and cooking oil.

- Cook until the beans are done (tender). Do not cook until the beans are overcooked or mushy.

- Add salt and remove from heat.

- Cut injera into small pieces and place in a serving dish.

- Pour the sauce and beans over the injera.

- Make sure the injera is well covered with the sauce.

Serves 4 to 6 people.

9

SPICY METIN SHIRO DISH
Yeberbere Metin Shiro Wot

INGRDIENTS

- Spicy Metin Shiro Dish
- Yeberbere metin shiro Wot
- 4 tablespoons metin shiro
- ½ cup cup water mixed with 1 table spoon cooking oil
- 4 cups of water (1 liter)
- ½ cup oil
- 1 tea spoon salt
- Preparation
- Add 4 table spoons of metin shiro to ½ cup water and 1 table spoon cooking oil.
- Mix them well

COOKING

- Place medium sized pot on high heat
- Add water and heat until water boils.
- Add oil and heat until it boil
- Add metin shiro mixture while stirring constantly
- Lower heat to medium high and cook for 30 minutes
- Lower heat to low and cook for another 10 minutes while stirring from time to time
- Add salt
- Lower to simmer and cook until oil surfaces
- Remove from heat

Serves 2 – 4 people

FRIED MEATS
TIBS

1

FRIED BEEF HUMP DISH
Whatela

Note: *This recipe calls for a dehydrated jerky. See Hump Preparation below to make ahead.*

INGREDIENTS

- 1 kilo (2 lbs. 3 oz.) dehydrated oxen hump
- 1 cup tej (Ethiopian honey wine)
- salt (to taste)
- Berbere paste (to taste)

HUMP PREPARATION

- Use dehydrated hump meat, or prepare by thinly slicing the hump meat and dehydrate it in a dehydrator before use.
- Sprinkle meat with salt, tej, and Berbere. The amounts depend on your individual taste.

COOKING

- Place frying pan on high heat.
- Add dehydrated hump meat to the pan and fry until the fat melts.
- Fry on the second side, but remove from the heat before all fat melts away.
- Serve immediately.

Serves 3 to 4 people.

2

FRIED BEEF OR LAMB SIRLOIN DISH
Gored Tibs

INGREDIENTS

- 1 kilogram (2 lbs. 3 oz.) beef or lamb sirloin or short loin meat
- 150 grams (5.3 oz.) clarified butter
- 30 grams (2 tablespoons) chopped shallots
- ½ tablespoons awaze paste
- 1 teaspoon black pepper
- ¼ cup tej (Egyptian honey wine)
- salt (to taste)
- pepper (to taste)

PREPARATION

- Cut meat into cubes of desired size.
- Sprinkle salt and pepper onto meat and mix well.
- Warm a bowl by filling it with boiling water for a few minutes, then empty.
- Place tej and awaze into the warmed bowl to create a paste.

COOKING

- Place a frying pan on very high heat.
- Add butter and let it bubble up.
- Add the meat and stir.
- When meat is brown on outside and medium rare inside, remove from heat.
- Place the seared meat in the tej and awaze bowl and mix well.
- Serve immediately.

Serves 3 to 4 people.

3

GRILLED CHUNK MEAT
Gibeta tibs

INGREDIENTS

- 100 grams (3.5 oz.) meat chunk (the upper part of the front leg)
- 100 grams (3.5 oz.) awaze paste
- 1 tablespoon black pepper
- 1 ½ cup tej (Egyptian honey wine)
- ½ teaspoon bile (if desired)
- salt (to taste)

PREPARATION

- Mix tej, awaze, and bile in a bowl and set aside.
- Sprinkle meat with salt and black pepper

COOKING

- Heat grill
- Add meat and grill until done (to your preference).
- When meat is darker on the outside and becomes juicy, remove from heat.
- Cover meat with tej mixture.
- Return meat to the skillet on low heat.
- Grill on both sides until a good aroma arises.
- Remove from heat.

Serves 20 to 30 people.

4

FRIED LAMB OR GOAT DISH
Yebeg Weyem Yifiyel Tebot Tibs

INGREDIENTS

- 1 kilo (2 lbs. 3 oz.) any lamb or goat meat (except ribs)
- 2 teaspoons black pepper
- 4 tablespoons clarified butter
- 2 large heads shallots, minced
- salt (to taste)

MEAT PREPARATION

- Cut meat into pieces of desired size.
- Sprinkle with salt and pepper.

FRYING

- Place skillet on high heat.
- Add meat and a proportionate amount of butter, depending on amount of meat used.
- Add butter and heat until butter bubbles and sauté.
- When meat is about done, add chopped shallots and sauté.
- When shallots begin to brown, remove and serve.

Serves 3 to 4 people.

5

FRIED LIVER DISH
Goubet Tibs

INGREDIENTS

- 1 kg (2 lbs. 3 oz.) beef or lamb liver
- 40 grams (2 2/3 tablespoons) thinly sliced shallots
- 10 grams (2 teaspoons) awaze
- 1 tablespoon clarified butter
- ½ teaspoon black pepper
- salt (to taste)
- jalapeño pepper, if desired
- 2 cups tej (Ethiopian honey wine)

PREPARATION

- Remove thin filament from liver.
- Cut into small cubes as desired.
- Rub cubes thoroughly with black pepper and salt.
- Mix tej and awaze in a bowl.
- Chop up jalapeño and set aside.

COOKING

- Place frying pan on high heat, add butter.
- When butter begins to bubble, add liver and sauté.
- Add shallots and jalapeño immediately and sauté with the meat for a little while.
- Remove from heat and place in a bowl.
- Add tej and awaze mixture to bowl and mix well.
- Place in a dish.

Serves 6 people.

6

FRIED TONGUE AND TRIPE DISH
Sember/Melas Tibs

INGREDIENTS

- 1 kilogram (2 lbs. 3 oz.) beef tongue
- 1 kilogram (2 lbs. 3 oz.) tripe (use the thick part)
- 1 large shallot, chopped
- ½ cup clarified butter
- 1 jalapeño or Serrano pepper, chopped
- 1 teaspoon black pepper
- salt (to taste)

PREPARATION

- Remove skin from tongue.
- Cut tongue into cubes of desired size.
- Sprinkle with salt and ½ teaspoon of the black pepper.
- Separate thick part of tripe from the skin.
- Cut tripe into cubes of desired size.
- Sprinkle with salt and remainder of black pepper.

FRYING

- Place skillet on high heat.
- Add ¼ tsp of butter, let it bubble.
- Add tongue cubes and shallots to the pan.
- Sauté until tongue is done and remove from the skillet; set aside.
- Add remainder of the butter to the skillet and let it bubble up.
- Add tripe.
- When tripe begins to puff, add rest of shallots and jalapeño and sauté for about five minutes.
- Mix the tongue with other ingredients in the skillet and sauté only for a few minutes (if sautéed too long, tongue will begin to toughen).
- Serve when well mixed.

Serves 6 people.

7

FRIED TRIPE AND LIVER DISH
Doulet

INGREDIENTS

- 1 lamb whole tripe and whole liver or ¼ beef liver and ¼ beef tripe
- Meetmeta (a chili pepper and spice mixture – see Glossary)
- 30 grams (2 tablespoons) clarified butter
- Salt (to taste)

PREPARATION

- Wash tripe with cold water and drain in a sieve.
- Cut into small pieces.
- Remove the filament from the liver and cut the meat into small pieces of a similar size to the tripe.
- Mix tripe, liver, meetmeta, and salt into a bowl and set aside.

COOKING

- Place a frying pan on high heat.
- Add butter and let it bubble.
- Immediately add the cut meat mixture and stir constantly for no longer than a minute to keep the meat rare (do not overcook liver or it will be dry).

Serves 5 to 6 people.

8

GRILLED BEEF OR LAMB RIBS DISH
Yebere Goden Weyem
Yebeg Goden Fim Tibs

INGREDIENTS

- 2 beef ribs or 4 lamb ribs
- 1 teaspoon beef or lamb bile (optional)
- 1 teaspoon black pepper
- ½ cup tej (Egyptian honey wine)
- salt (to taste)

PREPARATION

- Mix tej and bile in a bowl.
- Rub meat with salt and pepper.
- Prepare the barbeque pit or grill.

BARBEQUE

- Place meat on rack.
- When meat is broiled and ready according to your preference, remove from heat.
- Dip in bile and tej mixture and serve.

Serves 2 people.

9

RARE FRIED BEEF DISH
Yelewis Sega Leb Leb

INGREDIENTS

- 500 grams (1 lb. 1 oz.) lean meat
- 200 grams (7 oz.) clarified butter
- Up to 40 grams (2 2/3 tablespoons) Berbere paste and/or meetmeta (to taste)
- 1 teaspoon cardamom
- Salt (to taste)

PREPARATION

- Cut meat into very small cubes.
- Sprinkle meat with cardamom and salt, mix well.
- Mix well with Berbere paste and/or meetmeta.

COOKING

- Place frying pan on high heat, add butter and let bubble.
- Remove heated butter, pour onto meat, mixing as quickly as possible.

Serves 2 to 3 people.

10

SAUTEED BEEF JERKY DISH
Quanta Tibs

INGREDIENTS

- 500 grams (1 lb. 1 oz.) lean quanta (Ethiopian beef jerky)
- 500 grams (1 lb. 1 oz.) fatty quanta
- 2 tablespoons clarified butter

PREPARATION

- Take both lean and fatty quanta and break them up into small pieces.
- Mix together.

COOKING

- Place frying pan on medium high heat.
- Add both types of quanta to sauté and stir constantly.
- Add butter.
- When the fat of the quanta starts to melt, remove from heat. (If the quanta stays in the pan for too long, the lean quanta will become too dry and lose all of its fat.)
- Add more butter if the quanta is too dry while sautéing.

Serves 2 to 3 people.

GLOSSARY

The spices and mixed powders in this list are commonly sold in Ethiopian groceries.

ABSEET *A preparation mixed to use in Anebabero recipe. (See the instructions for Anebabero).*

AFRENGE *Jalapeño or Serrano pepper seeds prepared with garlic, ginger, white pepper, and salt.*

ALICHA KIMEM *Fresh ginger, and fresh garlic, and fresh sacred (holy) basil seeds.*

ALICHA SHIRO *A preparation of java beans, split peas, fenugreek, dried garlic, dried ginger, dried sacred (holy) basil leaves, cardamom, sacred (holy) basil seed, caraway seed, and long pepper.*

ASSA QUANTA *Ethiopian fish jerky.*

AWAZE *Jalapeño or serrano pepper prepared with garlic and rue seeds.*

BERBERE PASTE *A seasoned paste made by mixing 2 tablespoons of Berbere powder with ¼ cup lukewarm water.*

BERBERE POWDER *Jalapeño or serrano pepper prepared with rue seeds, garlic, ginger, sacred (holy) basil seeds, cardamom, cinnamon, cloves, caraway seeds, and salt.*

BERBERE WOT SHINKOURT KIMEM *A preparation of black cumin, caraway seed, garlic, ginger, and cardamom.*

CLARIFIED BUTTER *Prepared with fresh garlic, fresh ginger, shallots, cardamom, fenugreek, black cumin, long pepper, caraway seed, dried sacred (holy) basil seed, and true myrtle.*

COOKING OIL *Such as Mazola or other vegetable oil.*

ERSHO *A mixture of 3 tablespoons of tef with 1 cup of water.*

FALSE BANANA ROOTS FLOUR *Available at Ethiopian groceries (used in breakfast dishes).*

GLOSSARY

GENFO POWDER *Powdered barley grain (used in breakfast dishes).*

GINGER/GARLIC PASTE *Purée ginger and garlic separately. Mix one part garlic purée with two parts ginger paste.*

INJERA *A spongy, sourdough-risen flatbread traditionally made of tef flour. Injera flour is also made especially for this bread.*

KOULET KIMEM *A preparation of garlic, ginger, and dried rue seeds.*

MAKOULAYA KIMEM *A preparation of black cumin, dried garlic, dried ginger, cardamom, and caraway seed.*

MASTEKAKEYA KIMEM *A preparation of cardamom, cinnamon, caraway seed, cloves, and black cumin.*

MEETMETA *Red hot chili pepper prepared with cardamom and salt.*

MITIN SHIRO *Berbere powder prepared with garbanzo, split pea, fava beans, shallot, fresh ginger, fresh garlic, cardamom, and turmeric.*

NECH SHIRO *A preparation of java beans, split peas, garbanzo split peas, fenugreek, dried garlic, dried ginger, dried sacred (holy) basil seeds, cardamom, and caraway seeds.*

QUANTA *Ethiopian jerky. The recipes specify a type of meat (e.g. beef, fish).*

SEASONED OIL *Vegetable oil prepared with fresh garlic, fresh ginger, shallots, cardamom, fenugreek, black cumin, long pepper, caraway seed, dry holy basil seed, and coriander. See recipe at the end of this glossary. (See Addendum)*

SHENKOURT MAKULAYA *A preparation of dried garlic, dried ginger, and cardamom.*

SHENKOURT KIMEM *A mixture of dried garlic, dried ginger, cardamom, and caraway seeds.*

SHIRO FOR SPICY DISH *A preparation of java beans, split peas, garbanzo split peas, fenugreek, dried garlic, dried ginger, dried sacred (holy) basil seeds, cardamom, and caraway seeds.*

GLOSSARY

SHIRO FOR NON-SPICY (MILD) DISH *A preparation of java beans, split peas, fenugreek, dried garlic, dried ginger, dried sacred (holy) basil seeds, cardamom, caraway seed, and long pepper.*

TEF *A flour made from the tef grain. Whole wheat flour can sometimes be substituted.*

TEJ *Ethiopian dry honey wine.*

TENSIS *A preparation of soaked, sprouted, dried and ground wheat kernels.*

YEBOULA GENFO *Another name for false banana root floor.*

YETOM ALICHA DEREK KIMEM *A preparation of green cumin, white pepper, turmeric , and long pepper.*

"እናታችን ከልጅነታቸው ጀምሮ ለባልትና ሙያልዩ ፍላጎትና ትኩረት ነበራቸው"

"እራሴ መስራት ከጀመርኩ በሁዋላ የተዋጣልኝና የወደድኩት አሰራር እንዳይጠፋብኝ በፅሁፍ እመዘግባቸው ነበር "

Edwards Brothers Malloy
Oxnard, CA USA
September 17, 2015